S0-ARX-775

IT'S YOUR COMMUNITY!

By the same authors

The Book of Landscape Design
Color and Design for Every Garden
A Book about Soils for the Home Gardener

It's Your Community!

A GUIDE TO CIVIC

DEVELOPMENT AND BEAUTIFICATION

Henry B. Raymore, AIA, ASLA

AND

H. Stuart Ortloff, LA

M. BARROWS AND COMPANY, INC.

NEW YORK

Copyright © 1965 by Henry B. Raymore
and H. Stuart Ortloff

All rights reserved.

Published simultaneously in the Dominion
of Canada by George J. McLeod Limited, Toronto.

Printed in the United States of America.

Library of Congress Catalog Card Number 65–11493

HT
123
R3

)

MacN69

Sx

Acknowledgments

In preparing the material for this book the authors have not only drawn largely on their experience in planning and zoning, as well as their experience as architects and landscape architects, but have had able assistance from many other interested people. The material supplied by Mrs. Cyril G. Fox, chairman of the Executive Committee of the Pennsylvania Roadside Council, Inc., which is undoubtedly one of the most active councils and one which has accomplished great things, was of great value. Mrs. Wirt Darrow who has wide experience in the field of conservation was also very helpful, as were the suggestions of Mrs. Ralph Parker who is active in the program of civic beautification being carried out by various garden clubs with aid from Sears, Roebuck and Company.

As noted in the bibliography the official publications of the American Institute of Architects, *The Journal,* and that of the American Society of Landscape Architects, *Landscape Architecture,* were of great help not only in pertinent material but also as a source of inspiration.

Contents

Introduction

Speaking at a conference on Aesthetic Responsibility sponsored by the New York Chapter of the American Institute of Architects held at the Plaza Hotel in New York in 1962, August Heckscher, Special Consultant on the Arts to the President of the United States, deplored the ugliness we see all around us. Now the preoccupation of our lives (aside from the Cold War, of course) is not so much on "welfare," as it formerly was, he said, but on what might be called "the public happiness," a phrase that describes the satisfactions men find significant when they reach out beyond the search for security and for material benefits. To get rid of this ubiquitous ugliness is, therefore, one of our most pressing concerns.

The widespread lively interest in the development of the arts, even in the Congress, is a symptom of coming public awareness that the capacity to appreciate and enjoy, as well as the energy to create, exists in great measure among us. The maintenance of beauty and fitness in our surroundings, Mr. Heckscher stated, is wholly as important as other forms of culture in determining the quality of our society. The things men create outlast a living generation and carry the body of an age forward into the future and give life continuity. Yet these things, if not well considered and beautiful, cannot in any sense create a civilization. Only when men begin to take thought about what it is that they construct, and when the idea of beauty has found its place alongside the pressure of utility and of need, can civilization manifest itself.

In the past, to an amazing degree, the development of our communities has been left to chance. It seems that we did not care what our environment looked like. The hugeness of our continent and its abundance of natural resources led men to feel that despite what they might do to it in their small way, here and there, it would remain basically the same—an unspoiled, pleasant environment. We have assumed that private enterprise, left to its own devices, would somehow produce a desirable result. But now we are beginning to see that this has not happened. No, not at all.

As we look about us today we see how the bulldozer, the land speculator, the road-building engineer, the spread of suburban housing and the commercial development that follows in its wake, are destroying the countryside. The natural scenery may survive in the mountainous forest areas and in the widespread farming areas of the Middle West and South, but near our towns and cities it is fast disappearing. Our once neat towns and villages, whose individual entity was apparent, are joined together by great highways cluttered for miles and miles with cheap, shoddy commercial development. Behind these ribbon business strips stretch row after row of suburban houses, not all alike, but so nearly so as not to matter. Viewed from the highway or from the air these are seen to be wasteful destroyers of what might have been space arranged in an orderly way both for use and beauty.

In a recent editorial in *Landscape Architecture* the editor, Grady Clay, made a strong appeal to the "anti-uglies" to unite and form an American Civic Trust for the purpose of creating strong support for well-planned and beautifully executed public works. At present, he said, those who oppose an unsightly and ill-considered project are weak and divided. Usually they have to fight strong national or locally organized special interest groups. Those who oppose may include fanatics—how else do protest groups survive? And often protests are too late, inept, and emotional. Sadly lacking in positive suggestions or programs of their own, the opposers are often cast in the unpopular role of being "aginners."

It is surely necessary to oppose harmful proposals, but it is even more necessary to promote beneficial ones. If a sort of vacuum in civic thinking exists, it will be filled in one way or another. If good proposals are not brought forward, bad ones will fill the empty space.

Continuing with Mr. Clay's suggestions we, therefore, feel that the time has come for positive rather than negative action. Many resources lie ready to our hands. We have much to build on. A host of existing groups with a common interest in civic improvement, but which lack coordination, are already in being. We have leagues for the preservation of worthy institutions, scenes and objects, and many potential allies such as garden clubs and neighborhood improvement societies, citizens' associations for planning, open-space committees, conservation agencies of all sorts, local renewal societies and many others. Their efforts and money are often dissipated in driblets and their accomplishments seem meager in the light of the effort expended because they lack proper leadership in a common cause.

Mr. Clay concludes by saying that what is needed is a clearing house, a reference center, a source of guidance, advice and help. In other words *leadership*. Only thus can these diverse groups rise above local partisanship and become more than self-seekers.

To be successful any and all civic development and beautification projects need first to conduct a well-developed educational program to help overcome public apathy and to secure cooperation, not only by the public but also by municipal officials. To devise a good educational program, however, one must become fairly conversant, not only with the problem or problems under discussion, but also with the ways and means of achieving satisfactory solutions. One must know something about the workings of such official bodies as the Planning Boards, the Zoning Boards of Appeal, sometimes called Boards of Adjustment, Zoning Commissions, and other town, county and state agencies.

One must be aware of the political undercurrents moving below the surface of community life and be able to take these into consideration. No matter how worthy a project may be, if it lacks political appeal it will be treated with immense indifference by what we might refer to as the "Municipal Establishment."

Far too often many of the detrimental things that happen in a community occur because the general public is apathetic to the workings of the official agencies, not because "they couldn't care less" but because they feel they have little or no possible influence on the officials. In a democracy such as ours things come to pass largely through popular pressure. Well-organized groups can bring immense influence to bear on our legislative bodies, local, state and last, but not least, the Federal Congress. If enough people make their wishes felt through organized protests even our representatives in the Congress will pay attention.

Only by this means can the organized lobbies maintained by the billboard people, the anticonservationists and other self-interested groups be overcome. Without this the politicians, the real-estate developer, and other well-organized groups find little or no opposition to their schemes which easily gain official sanction and become matters of fact.

To help overcome some of these difficulties, to arouse people to the importance of preserving, enhancing and improving, not only the local environment but the regional and national one as well with their great natural and scenic resources; to encourage and publicize superior design in landscape architecture, architecture and urban development; to help prevent blight, neglect and uglification, and to try to help educate the public to support these goals vigorously, we have prepared the material which follows.

Henry B. Raymore, AIA, ASLA
H. Stuart Ortloff, LA
Half Hollows
Huntington, N.Y.

1. A Call for Action

Civic beautification begins with picking up the gum wrappers and cigarette butts around the benches in the courthouse square, but civic development may extend to such elaborate and monumental developments as the Capitol Mall and its environs in Washington, D.C., with the great Capitol at one end, the Washington Monument in the center, the Lincoln Memorial at the other end and the White House and the Jefferson Memorial on the cross axis, with the intervening spaces properly provided with roadways, walks and appropriate planting. It also begins with people, the ordinary citizen who lives in the community, and his appointed or elected officials.

A program of civic development and beautification can only begin, however, with the realization on the part of the citizenry that our communities are, today, largely ugly and unkempt. It is really extraordinary that the ubiquitous ugliness that exists all around us wherever man has established his towns and cities and has superseded natural conditions with man-made ones, is not more acutely realized and resented. We, that is most of us, take good care of the inside of our homes and of the grounds around them. Let there be an accumulation of trash in the gutter or, perchance, a dead animal in the street, how many of us will go out and deal with such a problem? More likely we will ignore it or call

1

the sanitation department or the police. After all they are paid to take care of such things, aren't they? We have come to depend altogether too much on the *authorities*, not only to do our chores for us but our thinking as well.

We not only permit, but are indifferent to, the ghastly commercial developments strung out along all the main highways leading into and out of our towns and cities. In fact we support them! We condone advertising signs and billboards in the name of free enterprise even when they desecrate the countryside or destroy or obliterate whatever architectural quality our buildings may possess. We permit, nay encourage, the construction of hideous high-rise apartment buildings in great groups to take the place of equally ugly, but less conspicuous, four- and five-story apartment buildings once decent but now degenerated into slums. The aim here is admirable. Who would not approve of getting rid of slums? But the results are often not only deadly dull but downright ugly. These projects remind one all too forceably of the regimented housing one sees east of the iron curtain. It is, of course, cheaper to build uniformly and without grace, but is it in the long run wise? What these projects do to the life of the neighborhood they replace is another and serious problem which we are tempted to discuss but which probably belongs elsewhere. However, one of the first steps toward civic beautification is to combat by every means at our disposal this all-pervading ugliness.

It is of little use to develop and plant a city square or small park if, all around it, ugly and decrepit structures of all sorts, signs, junk yards, and general untidiness are allowed to persist. How can one really justify the construction of an elaborate cultural or civic center when near-by rundown, over-crowded, obsolete slum dwellings are permitted to remain? The job should not be to beautify a spot here and there but to raise the whole level of civic housekeeping to a point where disorder is eliminated, ugliness done away with, and squalor transmuted into attractive, decent living and working environments. Mere tearing down and rebuilding is not enough. In fact it may do more harm than good since frequently in the process good, old things—buildings, trees, views—are destroyed and regimented mediocrity put in their place.

. Too much urban renewal has been undertaken without regard to the principles of urban design. Isolated projects, even though they may be worthy, do not necessarily add up to a well-designed or beautiful town or city. All parts of a viable, properly functioning community must be interrelated. If they are not, the community breaks apart into disassociated fragments, conflicting with rather than strengthening each other.

Such a program as we envisage is, of course, monumental in its scope. No one person or agency can encompass it. But unless we all, as citizens, individually or as civic and social organizations, municipal officials, municipal employees, property owners, merchants, industrialists, developers, agencies of the county, state and federal governments cooperate, only a diffuse effort, largely ineffective, will result. This fact tends to discourage those who realize the condition and feel that something has to be done about it. They do not know how or where to begin the attack on the problem and they feel frustrated. This is, of course, no valid excuse for abandoning the greater challenge. The fruits of victory are sweet and even though they may be interspersed with occasional failures, the interested citizen goes on just the same.

Often it is necessary to approach problems of civic development from many angles, simultaneously. The matter of cleaning the streets and public areas of the community must be handled by those employed by the municipality to attend such things, but someone must see to it that they do not neglect their duties. The matter of acquiring land for open spaces, municipal structures, recreation facilities, and other

civic purposes lies within the province of the municipal officials, usually the planning boards and the elected officers,
with referral, of course, to the voters who must approve the
various expenditures. The matter of how such lands are to be
developed, with what structures or facilities, so that both
usefulness and beauty are achieved, is the field of competence of the architects and landscape architects employed to
deal with such matters. The practical details of construction
lie in the field of engineering. Aid in financing urban planning and urban renewal comes from the state and federal
governments but they must be sold on the project before
such aid becomes available. And finally, nothing will get
done unless the citizens of the community are aware of the
existing conditions and ardently desire a change.

Far too often the average citizen is really not aware of
these existing conditions. In going about our daily tasks we
fail to see, let alone truly observe, the lack of beauty or even
decent order in our surroundings. We are concerned with
what affects our practical needs but fail to realize that the
appearance of our surroundings can be important in our
daily lives. If we would observe carefully, see more deeply
and more fully understand what we see, we would not tolerate the ugliness all around us. How often we pass billboards, junk yards, automobile graveyards, run-down or
burned-out buildings, or even uncared-for public property
and weed-infested rights-of-way without really seeing them!
"The eye is blind to what the mind does not see" is an old
proverb. Our sense of observation is untrained. In her auto-
biography Edna Ferber says she believes her keen sense of
observation was developed during her early years when she
worked as a reporter on a Midwestern newspaper. Perhaps
we should all go through a period of apprenticeship as re-
porters. In any event everyone should strive to develop a
keen sense of observation, not only to detect and deplore
ugliness in our environment but to get greater enjoyment out

of life generally. Along with observation a sense of discrimination must be developed. We must not only know what we are looking at but must be able to form some sort of judgment about it. Is it good or bad, beautiful or ugly, desirable or undesirable? The once meaningful word *taste* comes to mind. Without trying to define the undefinable may we say that discrimination and good taste go hand in hand and the more one has of both the better.

Not only will nothing get done until the people are aware of what exists, but neither will it unless they are also proud of their community, interested in it, and willing to make an effort and spend the necessary money to bring about desired improvements. Everyone is involved—property owners, bankers, realtors, developers, builders, industrialists as well as the various official bodies and, of course, the mythical man-in-the-street. He is the one we are really talking to. He holds the power as a citizen. He can, if he will, bring about whatever changes in our community environment that seem desirable, or let nature take its course and the devil take the hindmost, which he surely will.

It is encouraging to note here and there an awareness and a willingness to work and spend money for civic improvement. In dozens, perhaps hundreds of communities projects leading toward civic beautification have been undertaken. Many of these have accomplished wonders. In her admirable *This Land of Ours* Alice Harvey Hubbard lists and describes thirteen successful projects devised to preserve areas of natural beauty, twelve having to do with roadside improvement, twenty-nine dealing with municipal street plantings and the like, twenty-six having to do with special gardens and sanctuaries, and others dealing with community forests, schools, conservation projects and a host of others. The range of possible projects is so wide that almost everyone ought to be able to find a project in or near his community that will be of interest to him and on which he will be willing to work.

Often, however, isolated projects are poorly, or not at all, related to the growth and development of the community. Which is to say that any worthwhile project should be studied from the point of view of the community as a whole before it is finally decided upon and carried to completion. Only thus can waste and duplication of facilities be avoided. This may make for considerable difficulty because it is hard to obtain the necessary enthusiastic support for a project from all the influential or official people involved and because few communities have taken the time and trouble to sit down and really decide how they want their community to develop, for what purposes, and to serve what individuals or other interests. We hear a great deal about planning studies and Master Plans but less about their implementation and execution.

This is one of the phases of municipal planning that is so frustrating to a professional planner or planning consultant. It is almost impossible to get the interested groups in a community together to discuss and decide on community aims and purposes. Without such decisions, which should come from the community itself not from some hired planner or consultant, it is almost futile to prepare any plans for community development let alone anything as significant as a Master Plan.

Of course such bad civic housekeeping as dirty streets, decrepit, vacant buildings, weed-grown vacant lots, inappropriate and improperly located signs and billboards, can be taken care of without having to develop a complete community development plan and program, but any project that involves land acquisition, if it is to be satisfactory and of durable worth, any development or building for municipal purposes, or the construction of new streets and highways, or the widening of existing highways should be a well-thought-out part of such a community development program.

Some may find our use of the term *civic beautification* somewhat formidable. It may connote monumental buildings, decorative statuary, elaborately planted parks and public gardens, or civic and cultural centers all costing a great deal of money to create and more to maintain. This feeling stems, perhaps, from examples in the historic past like the Roman Forum, the boulevards and squares of Paris or Vienna, such modern examples as Brasilia and Canberra, to say nothing of the development of our national capital and its imitation in many of the states. Civic beautification may indeed go to such lengths but it need not. Most of our smaller cities that are not state capitals, and certainly the smaller towns and villages, have no need of such monumental installations. But they do need a general face lifting and the protection of existing amenities that make life more pleasant.

If only the disorder and extreme cases of inappropriate and ugly buildings were eliminated the improvement would astonish us. Once this state of comparative dishevelment were removed, we would be so pleased that we would be not only willing but anxious to go further with other projects to add an element of beauty to our now disorderly communities. In other words, we should begin with the elemental things like cleaning up and removing the worst offenses before proceeding to rebuild, enlarge and embellish. Though the program is formidable it is not, if taken step by step in easy stages, by any means impossible of accomplishment.

Not everyone is interested in the idea of civic development and beautification. There are many persons who are completely indifferent to their surroundings. They simply do not see disorder and ugliness, much less the need to do anything about them. As for such things as impressive municipal structures, monuments, or attractive plantings, they view these as pure luxury, all right for those who can afford them but by no means necessary to a satisfactory life. All one has to do is to look around to know that this is so. How else could such things as our contemporary school buildings, efficient though they may be, but drearily awkward in appearance, built to provide the most classrooms at the lowest possible cost and never mind what the result looks like; or our monotonous, glass-walled office buildings rising tier upon tier in our cities; or our roadside developments with their blatant gas stations, eateries and wayside salesrooms; or our gigantic, deadly dull housing developments, be permitted to come into existence? We do not expect to be able to reach these indifferent people, good citizens though they doubtless are, but we do hope to encourage and help the much smaller group of those who react violently against ugliness, who crave harmonious surroundings and pleasant neighborhoods, who delight in beautiful buildings, beautiful landscapes and works of art for their own sakes, and are willing to work so as to see that much more is accomplished.

It is these dedicated persons who must carry the burden of bringing about an improvement in the appearance of our communities. They cannot do it alone individually or even as a small group but there are many groups and agencies ready and willing to help if they are properly approached. These are, of course, the local municipal officials and the official boards. They must first be convinced that a proposed project is good in itself, soundly conceived, financially feasible within the resources of the community and, if possible, that it is politically advantageous. There is the Federal Housing and Home Administration (sometimes more familiarly known as the FHHA) which, through its aid for planning and urban renewal programs, can provide a great share of the money necessary to carry out a project. There are the local highway, police, and sanitation departments that can see that municipal housekeeping is improved and that the necessary maintenance of the completed project is supplied.

There are also many civic, fraternal and service organizations in every community that can be aroused to take an interest in projects for civic improvement and beautification and that can lend their influence and support to such endeavors. Finally, there are the numerous women's organizations, foremost among which are the garden clubs. Both the Garden Club of America, long interested in civic affairs, and the Federated Garden Clubs have, through their past and present efforts, achieved a standing of great importance and prestige in all matters pertaining to civic beautification. To these one should add the Women's Clubs, the League of Women Voters and many others who often initiate projects of great value. If, however, their endeavors are to be permanently effective they need the help and support of the official agencies and the general public.

Too often, unfortunately, an organization will undertake a project without adequate official support or adequate financial backing. Such a project, therefore, turns out to be either so small as to be ineffective, like planting a few shrubs around the town hall, or it may be sabotaged by uncooperative officials who, because they do not understand what is proposed, feel that it is only one more thing they will have to worry about. In nearly every instance of civic improvement much depends on the educational program which must precede the project itself. This must be thoroughly and clearly understandable. All questions raised must be answered without equivocation or evasion. Such an educational program should always be begun long enough in advance of any actual construction or the acquisition of any land to make sure that the necessary official sanction, the necessary funds, and as large a group of citizens as possible to serve as enthusiastic backers, have been brought together and organized for action.

In any civic project of considerable size and expense adequate professional advice from architects, landscape architects, or possibly engineers should be sought and obtained. The competent advice these professions can provide helps not only in the public educational program but in inducing the various official bodies to provide enthusiastic support.

Therefore any group of persons vitally interested in civic development and beautification must understand, themselves, what it is all about and what is possible and practicable. They need to have a better understanding of the historical development of towns and cities, the workings of the various municipal boards and agencies, and some of the reasons why we are at present in such dire straits.

Enthusiasm for a proposed project is never enough. With it must go a realization of how it fits into the life pattern of the community, what planning and what actual physical work will be required to bring it to fruition, and what will then become of it. And finally there must be a willingness to work indefatigably on the project until it is an accomplished fact.

2. The Urban Pattern

Historical Background

"In the beginning God created the heavens and the earth. And the earth was without form and void." Thus begins the great chronicle of Jewish history in the King James version of the Holy Bible. And so it was. Not until many thousands of years later, not until man had abandoned his nomadic habits and decided that it was more practical to live in one place and in a permanent dwelling did the idea of the community, and later the city, come into existence.

For purely practical reasons of convenience and safety man began to build his dwellings in groups which grew into the famous cities of ancient times. The great cities in the Nile Valley and the Middle East—Memphis, Thebes, Babylon, and Ninevah and later the Greek cities, and those of the Roman Empire. This development brought with it many problems. There was the matter of protection from enemies, hence walls with gates for egress and ingress that could be shut and locked in times of danger were built. There was the matter of water supply without which man cannot live, and hence wells were dug and later aqueducts were built and in some instances underground distribution systems were laid down. There was the matter of getting from one place to another. This eventually brought about the construction of

11

roads and, later, various types of transportation systems, both on land and sea. There was the problem of leisure and recreation, limited in ancient times, to be sure, merely to open space where people could congregate, but which eventually developed into parks, stadia, and other types of recreational areas as well as market places. All of these problems are still with us in one form or another. No city administration today can ignore any one of them, with the possible exception of walls for protection, although even today we are concerned with fall-out shelters for protection against enemies.

Once the city or town had taken a more or less permanent form, people became interested in improving their surroundings. Though it may seem that greater emphasis is placed on civic improvement today than was accorded in the past, the idea is by no means new. Herodotus tells us that as early as the 6th century B.C. the city of Babylon was a "planned city," as distinguished from other communities that had grown up casually at the crossing of two desert trails or caravan routes, perhaps around a well or an oasis.

Greek Cities and the Near East

The ancient Greeks of the 5th century B.C. paid a great deal of attention to civic beautification. They built usually around a hill or high rock on which they erected their temples. This was called the *acropolis,* meaning the high city. They lavished every skill they possessed to produce beautiful architecture embellished with sculpture and painting. When the word *acropolis* comes to mind we usually think of the one in Athens but this was not the only one. Every Greek city of any importance possessed such a site. The surrounding town may have been quite dull and even squalid but the acropolis was a many-splendored thing.

In their cities the ancients had the habit of building their houses right on the street line with few or no windows looking out, merely a blank wall and a stout door which could be securely fastened to prevent unwanted intrusions. This pattern is to be seen today in the ruins of Delos, Pompeii, and Herculaneum but it also persists in the more modern cities of the Near East, North Africa, and the Iberian peninsula. Inside the house the rooms were arranged around an open court known variously as an atrium, peristyle, or patio, which term still properly persists in Spain and Latin America but is often misapplied in the United States. These interior, open courts were usually embellished with a well or a pool (*impluvium*), and were planted with a few small trees for shade, shrubs in pots, and various medicinal and culinary herbs. Thus began the art of gardening which later developed into the profession of landscape architecture.

Another part of the Greek town or city that received great attention was the *agora* or market place, an open area to which the products of the surrounding countryside could be brought for sale. Quite naturally around such an area shops were built for the permanent display of goods or the performance of services. Later on people began to meet there to discuss the affairs of the day, or for social reasons.

Roman Cities

It is one of the clichés of architectural criticism to assert that the Romans, though good engineers and builders, never originated anything. They are said to have been great borrowers from and imitators of other cultures. They were indeed great ones for carrying off the statues and other art works that they found in the countries they conquered and setting them up in Rome and other Roman cities to beautify them, but perhaps more importantly, visibly to assert their prowess.

As in Egypt and other Near Eastern cities and also in

Greece and the Greek colonies, particularly in Sicily and southern Italy, and in Rome, the most elaborate buildings were the temples. These buildings were originally dedicated to the gods but later many were dedicated to the state and so we have the beginning of the sort of chauvinism which is causing so much grief in the world today. In Roman cities these buildings instead of being built on high places, such as an acropolis, were more usually built around an open space which was called a *forum*. This is the beginning of the civic center idea we hear about today. Around this area were grouped all sorts of buildings but all had some connection with the religious and civic life of the community and the area, the forum, became a place for public assembly and discussion. We often refer to a public debate as a forum although it may take place anywhere but in a forum area.

The basic plan of a Roman city was derived from their military camps or *castra*. The word has come down to us as Chester, either by itself or in combination, as in Dorchester, Colchester, Worcester, and the like. This plan consisted of straight streets and avenues crossing each other at right angles to form what we refer to as a gridiron pattern. Many modern cities follow this Roman example in their street patterns.

The Middle Ages

During the long dark middle ages that followed the collapse of the Roman Empire, after Rome had been sacked by the Goths, Vandals and other barbarian tribes from central Europe, very little progress was made in civic development or beautification as such. Those who lived in cities crowded together as closely as possible for protection behind high, fortified walls or built on islands as in Venice and Ravenna. No grand designs were promulgated but, during the latter part of the so-called middle ages, because of the intense religious atmosphere, great emphasis was placed on church, monastic and cathedral buildings and, although built for the glorification of God (and the bishop who had them built) they did add immensely to the beauty and importance of the cities in which they stood.

Perhaps not as much of this beauty was available to the average citizen of those times as would have been desirable since large portions of these buildings, being monastic foundations, were not open to the public; yet their exteriors could not be hidden and so everyone living in the city must necessarily see them as they went about their daily living. Their influence, therefore, was great. In few instances, however, were these buildings located with any thought as to their relation to the city as a whole. Often lacking in any sort of open space in front or around them they are still hard to see and frustrating to those who try to photograph them as anyone knows who has tried.

The Renaissance

By the middle of the 15th century A.D. things in Europe had settled down somewhat. It was an uneasy peace but at least the various principalities, duchies, and city states were not being constantly overrun by marauding bands of raiders. Florence was a peaceful and wealthy city state under the rule of the important and wealthy Medici family, while Milan had the no less important Sforza family, both of whom were interested in the arts and civic beautification. At this time, too, the expansion of the Ottoman Empire forced many Greeks to flee their own country and they came to Italy bringing with them their artistic inheritance and skills. This combination of peace, wealthy patrons, and skilled craftsmen generated the Renaissance which was to spread quickly over the whole of Europe and revitalize its art and its architecture.

With the use of gunpowder as a propellant at or about this period, strong city walls to protect the inhabitants were no longer effective. Hence, as towns and cities spread out from the confining walls into the surrounding countryside, people began to be concerned about how this expansion should take place with the result that highways began to be built to connect various towns and cities. This expansion also resulted in more room becoming available within the cities where obsolete structures and walls, being no longer needed, had been removed. These spaces were often used as sites for open squares decorated with groups of sculpture, fountains, and other decorative features. Trees were often planted and the open spaces became more parklike. Where the city walls had been, wide boulevards were constructed as in Paris, Vienna, and many other places.

Around the newly created open spaces public buildings were erected, recreating the old idea of the Roman forum but with a different form more nearly like the modern civic center. The architecture of this period was what might be called neoclassical since it was created by artisans steeped in the traditions of ancient Greece and Rome. It was characterized by a marked horizontality and the use of columns and colonnades in the classical manner, but it had a more exuberant decoration and less restraint than was common in classic times. It contrasted strongly with the predominantly vertical lines of the Gothic period that preceded it.

The Baroque City

The neoclassical city of the Renaissance soon gave way to the baroque cities of the 16th and 17th centuries. During this period monarchy was strong and wished to express its importance by monumentalism in architecture and the development of grandiose city plans. The straight-line gridiron pattern of streets, inherited from the Romans, that had been the vogue since cities escaped from within their enclosing walls, did not sufficiently express monumentalism to satisfy these ambitious monarchs. The simple market square dominated by the cathedral or the parish church gave way to much larger squares and plazas dominated by royal palaces and other imposing buildings, modern for their day, that contrasted with the Gothic churches which were by then considered to be old-fashioned. From these larger squares broad avenues radiated connecting various parts of the city and leading outward to the countryside. A good example of this type of development is the Place Stanislas at Nancy surrounded by 17th-century buildings including a town hall, hotel, fine arts' museum, theater, and courthouse with gorgeous wrought-iron railings, lead fountains, and trees. No church here. This square expresses the separation of church and state with the state growing in importance.

These baroque cities, of course, afforded more space and opportunity for civic beautification and embellishment than did the Gothic cities or even the neoclassical ones that preceded them. The basic pattern previously had been a jumble of narrow, crooked streets and alleys with no discernible logic other than an attempt to conform somewhat to topography and to reach all building sites. The neoclassical city had developed a pattern of straight avenues crossed at right angles by straight streets much as we see today in hundreds of American cities and towns. This pattern often defied topography as it does in San Francisco. It also often failed to provide a central focal point or core around which important buildings could be grouped. The baroque city combined the neoclassical straight-line gridiron pattern with a superimposed pattern of squares and *ronds points* connected with long, wide, straight avenues or boulevards which were generally diagonal to the gridiron pattern.

If it so happened that the city had been walled at an earlier period, this new pattern included wide streets or boulevards in such spaces so that there was a circular or ring road as well as the diagonals. The original L'Enfant plan for the city of Washington, D.C., is a perfect example of the baroque plan, prosaically lettered streets running in one direction and equally prosaically numbered streets running in the other with superimposed named avenues radiating from squares, circles, and small parks. These squares and other open spaces form the focal points of the design and they are frequently, and surely should be, accented by placing important buildings facing them.

Had the Industrial Revolution of the 18th and 19th centuries failed to develop, had the economy of Europe and the United States remained an agricultural one, it might have been possible for the baroque city to develop to its full fruition. It would have been very beautiful, spacious, clean and without slums though no doubt there would have been some poor and meager buildings. But this was not to be.

Industrial Cities of the 18th and 19th Centuries

With the invention of the steam engine and the steamboat the Industrial Revolution, already begun in the late 18th century, surged forward. This had a tremendous and devastating effect on civic design and civic beautification. Urban populations increased suddenly. Cheap housing for them was quickly run up without thought for the future. Factories dominated the waterfront areas of cities and what the factories did not appropriate the railroads did, so that nothing was left for use by the general public for rest or recreation. Of course, in the early days of the Industrial Revolution there was little time for rest or recreation. It was an era during which interest in the arts gave way to interest in making money for its own sake. Any other aim in life was looked upon with suspicion, and hence no one objected to the fact that everything was covered with soot and what beautiful buildings or sculpture might have existed were soon dingy and unsightly.

Typical of this era were the industrial cities of England like Manchester and Birmingham, and those of the United States such as Pittsburgh, that are only recently beginning to climb out of the morass into which they had fallen. The principal aim of this period was the creation of wealth and little or no attention was paid to the amenities of living. Industry was not only allowed but encouraged to eat into the very heart and core of our towns and cities and to foster among the working classes extreme poverty and squalid living.

The City Beautiful Movement

Of course such a condition could not endure and it brought about the rise of trade unions and the social legislation of the present day. The pendulum swings and one often wonders whether it does not sometimes swing too far. But the beginnings of the swing came not from the exploited workers themselves but from a movement among socially conscious people who sought to ameliorate the conditions of the workers. The "city beautiful" movement, abortive as it may have been, pointed the way toward a great deal of present-day civic beautification programming. Both in England and in the United States experimental "garden cities" were established whose aim was to remove the workers from the crowded slum conditions in the older areas of towns and cities and relocate them in new, modern, clean communities outside the cities, provided with the amenities of living and regulated as to growth. Letchworth, started in 1903, and Welwyn, both a few miles north of London, were planned and developed as garden cities. After sixty years they are both still attractive and well-cared-for communities and now that the trees have grown they look a lot older than they really are. But the idea of garden cities did not take firm root. Not many such communities were established and the centers of cities continued to deteriorate more and more rapidly so that even the outlying areas that had been built hastily and which were not well designed in the first place, soon became noisesome slums.

Development of American Cities

Meanwhile, in America many examples of deliberate town and city planning came into existence. As early as 1682 William Penn employed Thomas Holme, a surveyor, to lay out the completely new city of Philadelphia on an admirable plan which, though basically of the gridiron type, exhibited the device of four public squares balanced around a central one located at the crossing of the two main thoroughfares. This square was later obliterated by a monumental city hall so that today it no longer can count as open space. But the idea was a good one. Savannah likewise was a planned city from the beginning. It was based on rectangular blocks with a series of small squares strung like beads along what was intended to be the main thoroughfare.

In New England the pattern was almost always based on a central area of common land roughly rectangular, as in Boston, or elongated as in Hadley, Amherst, Longmeadow, and many other small towns. Around this open space were grouped the important buildings—the churches, the town hall, courthouse (if the town was a county seat), and the homes of the more well-to-do citizens. Many of these early towns still exist almost in their original form as at Old Deerfield, Massachusetts, and some have been reproduced as at Sturbridge Village in Massachusetts as a museum piece.

The South seems to have had its thoughts centered more on a public building, such as a courthouse or town hall rather than on a church as was the case in New England.

Gloucester, Virginia, is a fine example of this early pattern with its courthouse and accessory buildings set in an oval space in the center of the town. Williamsburg, Virginia, with its long malls leading to the capitol and the palace is another excellent example which has been meticulously restored for our edification and delight.

As the westward march of settlement took place many towns were laid out first on paper and then on the ground by surveyors. Most of them followed a single pattern consisting of two main streets crossing at right angles to each other in the center of the community at which point an open square was set apart in which a public building was built. These towns were so much alike, in fact, that training flyers during the First World War often mistook one for another and landed in the wrong places.

Such was the condition of town and city planning when the World's Columbian Exposition of 1893 opened its gates to an awe-struck public. Nothing like it had ever been seen in America, or perhaps anywhere else, since the days of Imperial Rome. Here was a classical city, brand new and bright, created complete on the shore of Lake Michigan. Its influence was incalculable. People from all over the country came, saw and marveled. And when they returned home they took a look at their own town or city and were horrified. A wave of proposals for new civic centers developed but, unfortunately, in their enthusiasm the proponents of these plans paid too little attention to ways and means. Many of the schemes, though beautiful, were too grandiose and much too expensive. Therefore, few were carried out and the enthusiasm for civic beautification suffered a setback. It was all too expensive a luxury best forgotten. After all, one had to think of taxes. But the idea did not die entirely and was to emerge again in our day as a more soundly based philosophy.

We hear today a great deal about the dangers inherent in

an "exploding population" and "urban sprawl." We constantly see the proliferation of suburban communities with their ill-considered subdivisions. We see valuable farm land taken out of production for these purposes and the alarming reduction of desirable open space. Yet far too often those who have escaped the crowded inconveniences of th' old town or city fail to realize that unless adequate steps a taken *now* they too, in the not too distant future, will aga be crowded in areas without the necessary amenities of op spaces and beautiful surroundings by a further proliferatic of other communities a little farther out from the congested areas. The key word in this is *now*.

3. The Modern American Community

The towns and cities of present-day America have been developed either on traditional gridiron or baroque plans, or have developed haphazardly on the basis of available land, demand for housing, or need for commercial and industrial expansion. In the early part of the 19th century canals and rivers influenced location, street pattern, and type of development. Later the railroads exerted a similar but even stronger influence. We see examples in cities like Syracuse, New York (canal); Marietta, Ohio (river); and Hagerstown, Maryland (railroad). Many towns developed as market centers to which farmers brought their produce for sale, hence a pattern of radial highways concentrating at the town center developed. Others like Brooklyn, New York, developed from a demand for housing rather than from commercial reasons and present another type of street pattern confusing to the unfamiliar visitor. Still other patterns were governed largely by the size and shape of individual properties.

All but the smallest of communities of whatever type tend to subdivide themselves into neighborhoods. These may be of many sorts and frequently they acquire informal names like Knob Hill, Country Club Heights, and the like that have a snobbish connotation, or Foggy Bottom, Shantytown, Skid

Row, or The Flats that are derogatory. Most of these names are descriptive and give some idea of the character of the neighborhood. Since people's social life tends to center within a rather small area, this division into neighborhoods is not a bad thing. When it is based on ethnic lines these separate neighborhoods often develop a cultural and social life of their own, quite distinct from that of the community as a whole. These different ways of life give piquancy and character to the whole community and can contribute significantly to its cultural life. It is only when such ethnic neighborhoods degenerate into slums from which residents wish to escape but cannot and into which people of a different background hesitate to move that conditions develop that create serious social problems of an undesirable sort. Many of our present-day racial problems stem from this basic difficulty.

Neighborhoods that are differentiated from each other by economic factors, rather than race or national origin, are a more recent phenomenon. In the past this sort of segregation did not constitute a community problem, but with the development of the huge suburban areas around our cities it has become much more acute. Because of zoning controls and the economics of land development many neighborhoods have been created in which practically everybody belongs to the same economic and age groups. This, we believe, is an evil that will have to be eradicated sooner or later. Before zoning controls and the great boom in housing that followed World War II occurred, most of our communities, especially the smaller ones, grew up in a manner that intermingled the well-to-do occupying relatively larger houses with the less affluent families occupying smaller ones. This sort of community possessed social strengths largely absent from a contemporary housing development or subdivision. The community tended to develop a desirable diversity within an over-all unity.

Community fragmentation tends to destroy the unity of the whole community, a tendency often intensified by the activities of local civic associations formed in each of the various subdivisions or developments. Their activities center principally on fending off what they conceive to be threats to their property values, or they indulge in excursions into local politics. They seldom seem concerned with the problems of the community as a whole and their members avoid involvement in community-wide programs of a charitable, cultural, or public-improvement nature. A clearly seen pattern of thought and activity characterized as *suburbanism* has emerged, something quite different from the ethos of the older communities. Some of the reasons why this situation has developed are that people moving into a new housing development arrive there simultaneously and suddenly and hence have no knowledge of the local community, and that most of them come from a large city where the individual tends to be lost in the mass so that they lack familiarity with small town ways or neighborhood patterns of living.

Most small towns, as distinguished from suburbs that have been built practically all at one time, originated in a small nucleus of a settlement at a crossroad, at a river landing, around a harbor, or other natural starting point. These nuclei became the core of the developing community and the thing that distinguishes a viable community from a synthetic suburban development is this core area which is an essential element of a real community. Around it the community develops and all phases of its life revolve. The continued health and development of the core area is of the utmost importance to the continued vitality of the community. Without it there is no focal point around which to coordinate the community's activities. It is in this core area that a need for civic development and beautification, so that its vitality may be preserved, generally exists.

In planning the community's development careful attention must be paid, therefore, to the strength of the core area. Nothing may be permitted to happen that will weaken it, and everything that will strengthen it should be encouraged. Not only should important civic, governmental, and cultural activities be located there but street patterns, parking facilities, open areas for rest and relaxation, and many other facilities should be provided so that it becomes an attractive and convenient area in which to shop, do business, or find recreation. As part of the city-beautiful movement some civic centers were established where these subsidiary facilities were not properly provided. These then became dead areas unattractive to the public which will go to them only when some special event or necessity requires. They fail to serve as effective community cores. At night downtown areas tend to be deserted and, unless a fairly massive program of enlivening them is undertaken, people will remain reluctant to go there after dark. And unless these downtown areas are well lighted, well populated, and well policed they will be avoided because they will be unsafe.

It is, therefore, desirable that such facilities as hotels, theaters, restaurants, and places of recreation be encouraged to locate in the downtown core of the community. High land costs often work against such a program and it may be necessary for the community to take a new look at its assessment roles to make tax concessions so as to induce desirable development. The fact that few such facilities have actually been provided in the older downtown areas in recent years by private enterprise and that most new hotels or motels are located on the outskirts of our towns and cities rather than in their core area indicates the force of these economic factors. Unless a reappraisal of the market value as reflected in the tax levies on downtown property is made, the deterioration of the downtown area will continue as will also the development of shoe-string commercial establishments along the outlying highways and in the residential neighborhoods not protected by adequate zoning controls.

The preservation of unity within a neighborhood is necessary if it is to become a strong social and cultural part of the community. One of the most disruptive forces in modern communities is the development of through highways or superhighways through, rather than between, neighborhoods. These facilities, when improperly located, can do more to destroy the social and economic life of a community, to say nothing of the disfigurement they cause, than any other thing. A case in point is the location of the New York Thruway approaching Tappan Zee bridge. It cut the community of Nyack in two with quite unfortunate effects. Protests by residents, however, availed little. The highway engineers won this round. Citizens should remain constantly alert to protest when proposals, especially for new highways, are made that disregard the interests of the local community neighborhoods.

Arbitrarily drawn school district lines also raise hob with neighborhoods. Where children living on one side of a street, for example, go to separate schools the unity of the street neighborhood is shattered. Adjustment of district lines to correct such situations is quite easy to accomplish. All that is required is agreement between the two school-district boards. People tend, however, to regard school-district lines as immutable, which they certainly are not. Of course readjusting school-district lines in an attempt to overcome the problems created by defects in the community's housing pattern is pretty silly, too.

A residential neighborhood needs to be a quiet enclave separate, to a degree, from the rest of the community with its own nucleus which may be a neighborhood school or a small retail commercial area, a group of churches, fraternal lodge buildings, or other facilities that tend to hold the neighborhood together. Not all such facilities have the same power to create community unity but all can serve to some extent and, in combination, they can be very effective. Without some focal points the neighborhood lacks any cohesive force to unite it and give it social significance. It becomes nothing but a collection of separate houses or apartment buildings that have little or nothing in common with each other.

A commercial or industrial neighborhood, on the other hand, needs activity and the presence of many people to give it life and add to its attractiveness. This means that while it is usually unwise to encourage residential uses in either a commercial or industrial neighborhood, cultural and recreational uses that will bring in people at times when the street and parking facilities are not in intensive use for commercial and industrial purposes, are highly desirable and should be encouraged. Churches, for instance, can properly be placed between a retail shopping area where adequate parking facilities have been provided so that these may be shared by the two sorts of uses, and a residential area. Stadia, bowling alleys, and other recreational facilities used at night can share streets and parking facilities primarily developed to serve commercial or industrial plants. School grounds can, and should, be used at night and during school vacations for recreational facilities for that part of the population not attending the school itself. More of this sharing than is currently the rule should be brought about.

The vast waste of resources tied up in idle school facilities is truly appalling, but only in recent years has it been possible for the general public to obtain use of them for anything but strictly school purposes. Local school boards tend to regard these buildings and grounds as their personal property to be used only in accordance with strict rules they may promulgate, forgetting that it is the public that has paid for the schools and that has a right to use them for any purpose that does not conflict with their use for school purposes.

In connection with a consideration of neighborhoods as social, cultural, and economic units the question of mixed uses is bound to arise. Many, if not most, current zoning ordinances are designed to prohibit rather than encourage mixed uses. In fact one of the strongest arguments in favor of a zoning ordinance is that under it the intrusion of undesirable uses into residential neighborhoods can be prevented. It is beginning to be realized, however, that this strict segregation of uses, residential here, commercial there, and industrial somewhere else, if at all, has not produced the ideal communities it was believed it would. Where this process has been carried to its logical conclusion we find all sorts of undesirable conditions developing. A residential neighborhood, if it is of any great size, needs a convenient shop or two, a gas station or other convenience facility properly located. A commercial neighborhood that contains nothing but retail shops is a dead area a great deal of the time, particularly in the evening and on weekends. It needs a theater, hotel, or motel and even, perhaps, a library or museum to enliven it and share the expensive facilities such as parking space, that would otherwise remain idle too much of the time. An industrial area can be a dreary wasteland when the plants are not in operation but it can often be brought back to life by a sports stadium, a swimming pool or a skating rink.

It should be the object of a good zoning ordinance to create harmonious juxtaposition of uses, not segregation and separation for their own sake. The interrelation of all these facilities in such a way that they do not interfere with each other or destroy the valuable characteristics of a neighborhood is one of the most difficult, but most important tasks of community planners. If they approach it with the idea of civic beautification uppermost in their minds, they will have before them a reliable criterion by which to judge what to permit and what to prohibit. Their job, and that of the whole community, is to see that their plans are implemented and that the desirable developments actually take place. One cannot create a park by drawing lines on a map. This merely indicates intent. From that point on it is a question of ways and means, public education, enthusiasm for the project, financing, zoning controls and a host of other planning procedures. The tendency is, once a zoning map has been prepared and adopted, to regard the task of planning as completed. As a matter of fact it has only begun. Zoning an area for commercial uses does not mean that stores will be built there. Establishing an industrial park does not mean that industry will immediately move in. Setting aside an area for expensive, moderate, or low-priced housing does not build housing. Economic pressures, by themselves, will no doubt bring about some of these desirable developments, but without guidance and encouragement from the community itself the process will be slow, sporadic and haphazard.

Not only will the adoption of a zoning map fail to stimulate the owners of property to develop their holdings in accordance with it, but very often indeed they find, at a subsequent date, that they cannot economically develop them as the zoning map suggests. This is a perfectly normal situation. No one, in making a zoning map can be sufficiently farsighted to tell how the community will actually develop. The map can never be more than an intelligent guess and an indication on the part of the planners that this is the way they would like to see the community grow.

The public, however, tends to regard the zoning map as something final and immutable and when applications are made for changes, sensible though they may be, a great deal of popular opposition often arises. Homeowners seem to think that a zoning map is a permanent contract between the municipality and themselves, a guarantee that the conditions existing when they bought their property will never be changed. If this were true, no community would ever be able to grow or meet the challenges of the future. When, however, zoning changes are requested or proposed, the residents of the affected area should be very sure that the proposed changes are really for the betterment of the area before acquiescing to the change. Many such applications for a change in zoning are made for purely selfish reasons without regard to the welfare of the community as a whole. That is probably why applications have come to be regarded by members of local civic associations and individuals as almost always something to be opposed. But there can be good and bad zoning changes. It is up to the citizens to realize clearly which are which and act accordingly.

Probably most people think of a neighborhood as primarily a residential area. What do we expect of such an area in terms of pleasant living? It makes little or no difference whether such a neighborhood is one of expensive homes on large lots or cheaper ones on small lots, or even if it is a district of apartment houses, row houses, so-called town houses, or whatever. For one thing people expect such a neighborhood to be quiet. This means that the street pattern should be such that it offers little or no temptation to cut through the neighborhood to get from one part of the community to another, or into or away from the community as a whole. In other words, a minimum of through streets and a minimum of entrances and exits from the neighborhood should be provided.

People expect the neighborhood to be attractive to look at. This means a well-designed street pattern with graceful curves where topography calls for them, with a minimum of pavement and a maximum of green verges, street trees and other planting where it is suitable. People expect a neighborhood to be well kept up. Vacant lots grown up to weeds and rough growths are most unattractive and should not be permitted to exist. People should maintain their own properties in a decent manner. This does not mean that they should necessarily spend large sums for elaborate foundation plantings and other front yard status symbols intended to impress the passer-by. In fact, many of these are in the worst possible taste.

An intensive program of education among homeowners, particularly in our newer suburbs, is needed. Simplicity and restraint should be the watchwords. A neighborhood where the front yards are treated simply and are well maintained is much more attractive than one where the homeowners have gone all out for the most elaborate and expensive treatments but have permitted these to outgrow their allotted space, or have neglected to take good care of them. If a neighborhood satisfies these three requirements: quiet, attractiveness, and good maintenance, it is more than likely to be a desirable place to live regardless of the size of the lots, cost of the houses, or personal characteristics, racial or otherwise, of the inhabitants.

Little regard has been paid in the past to the character of commercial neighborhoods. Most of the older ones grew bit by bit as opportunity for profitable development presented itself. Most of them, in the smaller towns and cities, grew up along main highways with the buildings placed right on the lot line and of a rather uninteresting type of architecture. Two- or three-story, flat-roofed buildings with shops on the ground floor and flats above were the rule. Latterly the upper stories are often omitted as fewer and fewer people are willing to live there.

Thus came into being the one-story "tax payer," a building frankly built as cheaply as possible to return a revenue sufficient to cover the taxes on the land until such a time as demand indicated the possibility of a more permanent structure. These have done nothing to enhance the attractiveness of our commercial areas. Nor has the practice of covering the upper story or stories of taller buildings, whose upper floors are no longer rentable, with sheet metal or other false front surfacing. Signs are a constant source of damage to the community's appearance. They obliterate whatever decent architecture may exist, they add confusion to the scene and, in many cases, they have become so blatant and so numerous that they cancel each other out and lose their effectiveness as advertising.

As a community grows, its commercial and industrial areas must also grow and, if the community is to remain in balance, at the same rate. This necessity often results in the enactment of changes in zoning that permit industry or commerce to eat into the older, residential districts and ruin them. Though tax revenues to the community are increased by the new industrial and commercial enterprises that come into existence in this manner, a balancing loss occurs because of the depreciation and obsolescence of the remaining structures. Often the loss exceeds the gain, to say nothing of the deterioration in community appearance that is caused. Before a community embarks on an intensive program to attract industry, however "light" it may be, into its midst it should carefully consider all the consequences. Industry and its associated uses not only bring in new revenue but they bring in also vast volumes of traffic with which the street pattern of the community may never have been designed to cope, and demands for types of housing that the community might not otherwise approve of. They also frequently demand auxiliary services that add to the cost of running the community.

If a program to attract industry into a community is contemplated, it is of the utmost importance that an area for such an expansion be carefully located so as not to disturb the existing core of the community or its residential districts. In most early zoning ordinances strips of property, generally about 100 feet deep all along every main highway were zoned for commercial use. Much of this was wishful thinking since few communities so zoned would ever require that much commercial space. As a result building took place in a spotty, haphazard way and many of the main thoroughfares in and approach roads to our various communities were permanently ruined by cheap, meretricious commercial development. Once this sort of thing has started it is most difficult to stop its spread. Sometimes unoccupied commercially zoned land can be zoned back for another more suitable use but property owners invariably oppose such changes. Zoning has a tremendous effect on property values and when a piece of land is zoned for commercial or industrial use, its speculative value immediately rises. The taxes it pays are often based on this inflated value. When and if an attempt is made to rezone the land to a use that offers fewer speculative possibilities the owner is immediately outraged, declares that he is being persecuted for no good reason, and proceeds to defend his "rights" in every way that is open to him.

Commercial districts of the older type also suffer from other diseases. In many places obsolete or run-down, tumbledown buildings are allowed to remain, and where they are removed and the area devoted to parking facilities, the area becomes fragmented, less attractive, and ultimately less successful economically. Many such districts need a course of face lifting which should take the form, not only of the reconditioning and modernization of existing sound structures, but the replacement of obsolete ones, not with small parking lots which are almost always inefficient, but with small parks or parklets, quiet places where shoppers or office workers can stop, rest, and relax for a few moments during the busy day. Such a use not only adds to the attractiveness of a commercial area but serves a definite social need.

In one small town we know of a small area was made available after the destruction by fire of a group of old, downtown buildings. This was quite inexpensively improved by paving the area with gravel, placing a few benches and beach umbrellas and some planting—a few flowers in boxes, shrubs, and a couple of small trees. The place was delightful and much used as a meeting place and a rest area for shoppers. Places such as these add immensely to the beauty and agreeableness of a downtown commercial complex. Of course, in a larger town a real pedestrian mall can be established. This is, however, a special type of development that will be discussed at length later.

New commercial districts are nowadays mostly of the shopping center type, ranging from the huge ones like Northland, Whitman, Roosevelt Field, and Shoppers World to the small unit of a few retail shops, hastily and cheaply built, revolving around a supermarket, set back from the highway and surrounded by a desert of asphalt parking space. Most of these, even some of the really large ones, are architecturally deplorable and, from the point of view of community attractiveness, sorely lacking in the amenities. Here is an opportunity for those who would improve their community's appearance. It should be seen to, by one means or another, that these shopping areas are redesigned for greater attractiveness and better maintained.

Except to clean them up, control signs, and police them effectively, not a great deal can be done about such shopping centers as are already in existence. But before any more are built the community would be well advised to institute zoning controls that will assure that these facilities will not only be convenient but more attractive to look at. Such controls are well within the legal powers of the community. Building setbacks, a desirable ratio of parking space to sales space, adequate lighting and, above all, adequate and well-maintained planting areas both to dress up the area itself and to screen it from neighboring residential areas can be reasonably demanded. The requirement that all plans for such facilities be passed upon and approved by a competent landscape architect should be incorporated in every zoning ordinance. If the community has established an architectural board of review, something can be done about the appearance of the buildings as well.

Industrial districts have always been regarded as the least desirable ones in the community and hence, in most older zoning ordinances, the industrially zoned land was usually located along railroad rights-of-way, dock areas and the like, or were parcels of land that seemed unsuitable for either residential or commercial development. All land-use regulations tend to follow the principle of the most profitable use—*for the owners*—of the land in question. Zoning ordinances do not necessarily reflect what the best use, from the point of view of the community's inhabitants, might be. Until a change in viewpoint is brought about, zoning will continue to be of little assistance in bringing about community beautification.

Of course, before the widespread use of electricity to power industrial machinery, a valid objection existed to locating industry near residential areas. Not only were the buildings ugly but a great deal of noise, smoke, and fumes were produced. This is no longer true to any such extent. Many modern industries operate quietly without smoke or fumes and hence they are, to this extent, compatible with residential areas. The tendency toward one-story rather than multiple-story buildings and a greater appreciation on the part of industrialists of clean, modern factory buildings has also tended to dispel the opposition to such facilities being located near, or even among, residential neighborhoods. The traffic problems generated by industry, however, remain and they can mitigate against its location where, except for this drawback, it would be desirable. Pride in the appearance of their factories on the part of many owners has led to their installing wide lawns and plantings that enhance not only the buildings themselves, but the community as a whole.

These tendencies should certainly be encouraged. Zoning ordinances frequently attempt to do this with considerable success.

In older communities any waterfront land they might encompass has been almost always pre-empted by industry. This was natural enough when shipment of freight by water was the prevailing mode, but this is no longer true. Some things, like oil tanks, need to be near water since oil is still transported by barge, but most industries are just as happy inland. Hence these waterfront areas can, and should, be returned to public use. Parks and promenades along them, swimming pools where water pollution is not a problem, places for outdoor concerts and other cultural activities can easily be provided for in these areas. The Franklin Delano Roosevelt Drive with its auxiliary parks and playgrounds in New York City, Chicago's magnificent lake-front developments, in West Virginia Charleston's Kanawha River project, Boston's Fenway development and many others show what can be accomplished.

4. Traffic and the Parking Problem

In every community in the land, large or small, traffic and how to manage it is one of the most pressing municipal problems. It has an important bearing on civic development and beautification because many of the expedients adopted to deal with this problem have caused, and are continuing to cause, uglification.

Perhaps in small communities the problem does not seem as great as in the larger ones, and hence it may be brushed aside, but even in the crossroads hamlet or the residential subdivision some provisions have to be made for managing traffic, including both moving and standing vehicles.

Americans are inordinately fond of the automobile which has become a status symbol of great importance. Not only do we drive the biggest and the fastest cars in the world, but it is the desire of most of us to own at least one automobile and many American families own two or more. The possession of four or five is by no means unknown. We no longer walk anywhere. To go to the corner store for a small purchase we get the car out and, more likely than not, we do not put it back in the garage again for we might want to go out again in the next hour or so for a major or a minor errand. So the automobiles not only have to be housed for the night but a place for them to stand during the day must be provided.

We were all brought up with the notion that the streets

were public property and that we could drive, walk, or stop on them anywhere or any time we saw fit. When we drove the horse and carriage into town, or rode in on a bicycle, we naturally stopped as near our destination as possible, tied the horse to a hitching post or leaned the bicycle against the front of the general store, and thought no more about it. Later we stopped the automobile along the curb in the same manner. But soon there were just too many automobiles for the amount of curb space available. In fact, those who got to town early pre-empted the space and later arrivals found it impossible to stop and transact their business without walking considerable distances.

Parking Controls

Parking meters to limit the use of curb space, and provision of off-street parking areas for automobiles for shorter or longer periods of time, had to come into being. These were revolutionary ideas and it took a long time for them to be generally accepted. Even today the question of whether or not to install meters or where a parking lot is to be built, and most importantly who is to pay for it, can literally rend a community asunder.

Parking meters are often sold to a community on the assumption that they will provide revenue over and above the cost of their installation and maintenance. They often do, but this should not be the primary reason for their installation. Their purpose is to limit and regulate the use of parking space. One can hardly quarrel with this when meters are installed in congested, commercial areas, or on residential streets adjacent to such areas, or near railroad and bus stations or anywhere where all day parking is customary. But the use of parking meters to produce revenue or prevent curb parking in residential areas, just because the abutting owners like to see the street empty of parked cars or so that they can pull up in front of their own houses whenever they like, seems unreasonable.

Curb parking, though traditional, is generally not really a good thing. When both sides, or even one side, of the street are parked solid with cars the flow of traffic is not only interfered with, but the signs and show windows the merchants have been to such expense to create, are largely wasted. The passing motorist can see nothing of them. Not only that but cars backing in or coming out of curb parking spaces create a hazardous condition resulting in accidents, to say nothing of the delays of traffic while a driver parks his car or emerges from the curb space.

At certain points in a commercial area, as in front of a Post Office, theater, hotel, or library, cars should be permitted to stop and be parked for a matter of ten to fifteen minutes. It would be an excellent thing if, in such locations, the buildings were set back sufficiently to permit the roadway to be widened so that cars could pull out of the traffic to make these stops. The errands one does at such places are usually short, one does not intend to linger, and one doesn't like having to go any distance to find a parking place and then walk back, nor should one have to do so. Banks have finally awakened to the fact that the business of a majority of their customers is usually a short affair and are now providing drive-in windows. Modern hotels and motels provide off-street space for parking while registering. Theaters and libraries ought to but as far as we know, they do not provide facilities for short stops. Post Offices are the worst offenders. The federal government, which controls these buildings either through ownership or lease, seems not to have thought of the parking problem at all. They provide loading bays for their own mail trucks but nothing for the customers. Libraries which seldom provide long-time parking facilities for those doing research or making lengthy visits to them should certainly do so.

In suburban residential areas curb parking should be prohibited and we see no reason why this cannot be done right away in most places. Almost everyone has a driveway into which cars can turn and be parked or additional space along the driveway can easily be provided. Prohibiting parking on residential streets would do a great deal to improve the appearance of our communities, to say nothing of increasing traffic flow and safety.

Parking Lots

Off-street parking areas, either in the open or undercover, provide space for cars, but they are all too often a blight on the community's appearance. A parking lot need not be ugly. If the services of a competent architect or landscape architect were employed in laying out such facilities a great improvement in their appearance would result. Where, in cities or even sometimes small towns, a building or a group of buildings have been torn down to create a parking lot why is it that the adjoining buildings are always left in a raw, ugly condition? Why cannot these walls be refinished with brick, stucco or other suitable material? Why cannot ivy or other vines be planted on them? Why cannot ugly signs and billboards be prohibited? Even the surface of many of these lots is often bad and puddles and potholes abound, fences are delapidated and the "office" a mere shack. Those who would beautify their community could do worse than start to work on parking lots.

No matter how many such lots are provided, whether by private enterprise, merchants' associations, or by the municipality itself there are never enough of them. Traffic proliferates faster than parking areas can be provided. It is, therefore, wise for each community, with this fact in mind, to provide for the future needs by adequate zoning controls that will prevent the use of property ultimately to be used for parking purposes for any other permanent improvement. A long-range plan is necessary so that, when the time comes, the areas will be available where they are needed most. Another device is to require, under the zoning ordinance, that all commercial and industrial buildings provide adequate off-street parking.

In the smaller towns and in the outlying areas of the larger cities parking lots are usually constructed on vacant land or as a part of a slum-clearance program. Villages frequently acquire the rear portion of the lots on which their main-street buildings stand and turn this into parking areas. This is a sound idea as far as it goes. Even new municipal parking lots created in this manner, however, are seldom developed attractively. Much more than is customarily accomplished could be done by fixing up the rear of these buildings facing the parking lot. This sort of "urban renewal" as it were, is inexpensive but extremely effective in bringing customers to the business buildings so treated and in making the use of the parking lot itself more popular. Professional help on the design of these lots, and a cooperative effort by the property owners under the guidance of a competent architect, would make these areas much more attractive. Incidentally, they would be used with more confidence, especially by women shoppers who dislike very much to use a parking lot that is reached only through a back alley and from which they must walk quite a distance to reach the shops of their choice. Furthermore, if the shops would construct rear entrances it would reduce walking and if show windows could be introduced they might help to attract customers. The American shopper, man or woman, today will not walk far. He will drive miles to find a parking space near enough to a shop or restaurant of the sort he seeks rather than walk a couple of blocks to one right near home. Absurd, perhaps, but true.

Parking lots may be acquired in a variety of ways. The

municipality may exercise its right to condemn land for this purpose. If it appears that a parking lot can be operated profitably, individual property owners may decide to use their land for this purpose. Sometimes, in desperation, merchants can be induced to cooperate in the acquisition, development, and management of parking lots in commercial areas. In newer shopping centers parking is automatically provided as a part of the project as the promoters of these realize that in order to attract customers their facilities must be adequate and convenient. In older commercial areas, however, it is often difficult to get the merchants or property owners together on any such project. They still think the customer ought to take care of his own parking problems, perhaps with the assistance of the municipality, but feel that it is surely no concern of theirs. This is very shortsighted and many an older commercial area is suffering deterioration and loss of business because of it.

Parking lots need not be ugly. We have already said this and say it again. Although it is true that a lot designed to be reasonably attractive will probably not accommodate quite as many cars as the one designed purely for the purpose of crowding in as many cars as possible, the loss need not be great and the gain in popularity is tremendous. Nothing detracts from the appearance of a downtown area as much as parking lots tucked in between buildings without any logical pattern and without anything having been done to make them attractive and easy to use. All big cities suffer from this blight to a greater or lesser extent and the small towns are beginning to succumb to it. Citizens should take note of this problem before it becomes acute and see to it that the necessary steps are taken to avoid the damaging effects these numerous, small, ill-designed parking lots can have. It is often much wiser to use these small vacant lots for parklets for people instead of for car parking.

In parking areas constructed in connection with most

modern shopping centers of any size space is provided for a certain amount of shrub and tree planting, even an occasional flower bed. The same sort of thing could be well applied to municipal or privately owned parking lots, though this is less often done because of the high land values and the need to accommodate as many cars as possible. Nevertheless, any parking lot, if it is not to damage the community in which it is located, should be made attractive as well as efficient.

These tree and shrub plantings must be carefully designed so that there will be sufficient room for the plants to grow naturally and not have to be chopped back to keep them out of the way of cars, and so as to reduce the required maintenance as much as possible. In the South particularly, and even in the North, the shade provided by trees or light, airy attractive awninglike structures in parking lots will make them more usable during hot, sunny weather, as everyone who has had to get into a car that has stood for a time, shut up in the sun, well knows. The trees used to provide shade, however, must be of the sort that will not drip sap or drop flowers or fruit onto the cars, and they should be sufficiently high branched so that even when laden with rain or snow they will not hang down so low as to interfere with parked cars.

For a garden club to undertake the beautification of such an area on its own responsibility and merely with the consent, but not the financial support of either the parking lot owner or the municipality, is a risky business. Usually the funds available are insufficient to do a good job and the problem of maintenance is too often left unsolved. Garden clubs can, however, often bring about the improvement in the appearance of parking lots by offering an award of merit to those that have made their lots more attractive through the use of plants.

Solutions of the parking problem, other than open parking

lots and street parking, like underground parking areas or parking garages are admissible. They take care of more cars than open lots do, and they are less conspicuous. But they require attendants to park cars and hence their use is more costly to the motorist. Such facilities are particularly appreciated in the colder parts of the country and are applicable to the larger urban centers. Sometimes, as in Boston and Pittsburgh where the parking areas have been constructed under the Common and a public square, two purposes are served—parking and the preservation of open space above.

Parking garages of the pigeon-hole type where automatic operation is featured—have not proved very popular as yet, perhaps because the operation is not fully perfected and understood—or parking towers and other types of garages appearing more and more in our cities are useful but often ugly, especially when they are built with open sides exposing the parked cars to view. In one small city in Georgia a glaring example of this has been built with the object of drawing back to the downtown area shopping traffic from a new suburban shopping center. It has not only failed in its purpose but stands as an ugly blot on the downtown cityscape.

At times most communities become rather frantic in their search for suitable areas for parking. The temptation is almost irresistible to turn the lawn around the city hall into a parking lot, or the village green or some other open space is nibbled away at the edges or completely desecrated. This temptation should be most vigorously resisted and every civic organization and every articulate individual in the community should rise up and fight any such proposal until it is finally defeated. Desirable space may be scarce but it is not nonexistent and never, but never, should a public park or square that is needed to beautify the community and make it a more desirable place in which to live, and that is doing its job, be encroached upon or used for any purpose whatever other than that for which it was originally intended. Highway engineers particularly love to run their highways along the edge of a park, taking "only a few feet that never will be missed." Well-intentioned people try to establish museums, restaurants, and other worthy structures in an open space or park. After all "they will add interest" to the scene, they claim. Encroachments for these and other similar purposes are common. Resist, resist, resist! Keep the parks and open spaces inviolate!

This is easier said than done. It is difficult to arouse people to take action against these proposals especially when the encroachment appears to be slight, harmless, or at a remote location. Those promoting such encroachments have a tremendous advantage. They are on the inside, part of the "establishment," and they can perfect their plans quietly and often secretly until, having obtained small concessions here and there, the project has progressed to a point of no return. Suddenly the community becomes aware of what is about to happen, but it is too late to prevent it.

Every community, however, has in it some old, obsolete buildings that no longer serve a purpose. It is these sites that make desirable parking lots, especially if enough buildings are removed to make the area big enough to be developed in an attractive and efficient manner and, as has been suggested, where the business blocks are deep, it is frequently possible to provide adequate parking in the rear of stores and offices.

Mention has been made of the dislike for walking that most Americans have. Surveys indicate that the estimated distance a customer will walk is between 100 and 500 feet. A fair average is 300 feet. Employees will, of course, walk farther, not because they want to but because they usually have to, as most parking areas in a business district are restricted to one- or two-hour parking.

Surveys have also indicated that the proportion of parking

area to sales area should be about 300 square feet of parking for every ten expected customers or every five employees. Such a ratio is very difficult to achieve in most older built-up communities. Other formulas are in use but since there are so many variables in the situation none of them is completely reliable. Some municipalities arbitrarily require off-street parking areas of a specific size for all commercial buildings regardless of use. This is often unreasonable and it infuriates builders. The word here is to beware of rigid requirements bureaucratically administered in this field, or any other.

This sort of zoning provision, though its purpose is admirable, is difficult to write or enforce in such a way that it accomplishes the desired result and avoids unfair treatment of the owners of commercial property. When a large or small building is proposed for a large lot, compliance with on-site parking requirements is easy but when a building is proposed for a small lot held in separate ownership, compliance may prove to be very difficult, if not impossible. Before adopting such a zoning provision a community should look carefully into the matter of property ownership in its commercial areas to see just how such an ordinance might be expected to work.

5. Moving Traffic and Its Control

There are two kinds of traffic with which a community has to contend—vehicular and pedestrian. Of the two the former is the sort which has always created problems affecting both the attractiveness of a community and its efficiency as a place in which to live and work. Pedestrian traffic, though important, is less troublesome.

Vehicular traffic, in turn, is of two sorts: through traffic which consists of vehicles passing through a community to a farther destination and local traffic within a community. These sorts may be further subdivided into through traffic that might like to stop, if an opportunity presented itself, and then move on, and local traffic that desires to go but a short distance, more or less within the neighborhood—local residential traffic one might call it—and local traffic that wants to go from one part of the community to another for shopping, business, or social reasons.

Through Traffic and Highways

For years it was vehemently maintained by commercial interests that through traffic should pass through the main street of a community so that travelers would stop and make purchases or conduct other types of business. Merchants fought bitterly in the twenties and early thirties to prevent highways being rerouted outside their commercial areas. They also fought parking regulations and restrictions on such streets and insisted on parking their own vehicles there as well. Of course this resulted, as anyone might have predicted, in few travelers stopping in a community. They could not because there was little or no place to stop. They tended to stop, if at all, outside the community, thus bringing about the proliferation of roadside business establishments on all major highways leading into or out of the community. Unfortunately, most of this development was unplanned and cheaply constructed with the result that we have and are faced today with the problem of what to do with our roadsides to make them attractive instead of ugly. Once highway planners began to realize what was happening they began to reroute highways outside communities and to try to control what could be built along them and how and where access to them might be permitted. Few travelers nowadays stop in a community except at a hotel, motel, or garage, and such stops tend to be of fairly long duration. Progressive hotels are now providing off-street parking facilities, motels and garages always have done so. This lack of parking space is, undoubtedly, one of the contributing factors to the loss of business of hotels to the new motels outside the town.

When heavy, through traffic, particularly truck traffic, is permitted, a definite deterioration of the streets over which it passes occurs. (Delaware Avenue and Genessee Street in Buffalo are good examples.) Residences on such streets soon give way to rooming houses and commercial buildings, then high-grade retail shops move out and other, less desirable uses move in. One of the first steps toward civic improvement is to get through traffic out of the central business district of the community, however large or small this area may be and, of course, strive to keep it out of established residential areas as well. Where this is not done blight inevitably sets in.

The concept of through highways out in the country, passing through no towns and avoiding established residential communities is a sound one. The present federal highway system now under construction all over the country is a wonderful thing, even though there is, apparently, no definite over-all pattern and it is fabulously expensive. But it has its drawbacks and difficulties too. If such a highway system is not laid out with consideration as to what its effect will be on the countryside through which it passes, it can do a great deal of damage particularly where it runs near a town, village, or city. No such highway should be permitted to divide residential or other types of neighborhoods to their disadvantage. If, however, it runs between neighborhoods rather than through them, it can serve a useful purpose in community design. Such highways should be related to the topography through which they pass, avoiding extremes of cut and fill that scar the countryside beyond repair. Access to such a highway should be provided only at specific points and, if there are homes or business establishments along it which it must serve, a service road parallel to the main traffic artery must be constructed. Too many through highways are designed by engineers who pay little or no attention to the aesthetics of design. They are, usually, overly concerned with the shortness of distance and the alignment of the roadway. Sometimes it would appear that they are not very much concerned with costs.

At most intersections of these superhighways with older roads, the right of way has been widened considerably to provide for adequate approach and turn-off roadways. The spaces between these, usually left in rough grass, provide an ideal place in which some decorative planting can be done to relieve the tedium in the long, monotonous road. This planting, however, must be most carefully designed so that it neither obstructs the vision of motorists entering, leaving, or just driving along the highway, nor is of such a nature that it unduly attracts attention. This is no place for a rose garden or other detailed plantings that have to be seen closely to be appreciated. Masses of color can be used occasionally but they must be real masses not dots and dabs. Maintenance must also be carefully considered as these plantings are unlikely to receive much special care. A further discussion of this problem appears under the discussion of Roadside Development.

Much more can and should be done along major highways to create points of interest and to help relieve the dangerous monotony caused by the unrelieved winding ribbon of seemingly endless concrete. These limited access highways are of three easily distinguished types. The first to come into being, and still the most attractive, are the parkways. The Fenway and the Felsway parkways in Boston were probably the earliest of these. Later came the Bronx River, the Hutchinson, the Taconic in New York, the Garden State in New Jersey, and the Interstate in New Jersey and New York among many others in other states. The principal characteristics of such roads is that they are designed primarily as pleasure drives, not as trunk highways. Hence they are designed for moderate speeds and decorative planting along them is featured.

Expressways and turnpikes on the other hand are designed primarily to move as much traffic as rapidly as possible from one place to another. They are designed for higher speeds than are the parkways and the planting along them, although provided to some extent, is not featured. The third type of superhighway is the federal system that exhibits the principal features of the turnpikes but is toll free. In one respect they differ from the parkways and turnpikes in that no service areas are to be provided along them and that, if the state legislature so ruled, no billboards, except under certain circumstances, may be erected within 660 feet of the right of way. Planting along such highways, though badly needed, has not, so far, been provided to any significant extent.

Planting along any of these superhighways should generally be in bold masses with, of course, a few outstanding trees all set well back from the traveled area. There is the interesting possibility of grouping the various plant materials together into pleasing, harmonious compositions by paying careful attention to form, texture and color. Furthermore, highway engineers should give greater attention to the preservation of native growths which, according to the facts of ecology, do better with far less care than material that is not indigenous. In some sections outstanding work on planting development along parkways has been done, and a study of these examples can indicate what has been successful and may be copied or used more extensively. The possibilities have by no means been exhausted nor has enough money to bring about this sort of beautification been provided.

Along such roadways including the great turnpikes, the federal system, and the parkways, many more places to pull off out of traffic to stop, rest, and enjoy the scenery should be provided. Driving at high speeds is monotonous and fatiguing. Drivers simply must stop now and then to get out and stretch and be able to readjust their eyes to a stationary scene as a contrast to the constantly changing kaleidoscope of fast-moving images that confront them while driving. Service areas every thirty miles or so along turnpikes are far too infrequent to serve this purpose. Furthermore they are likely to be busy, bustling places not especially conducive to relaxation. What are desperately needed are more rest areas (pull-offs or lay-bys, as the English call them) where a driver can get out of the main stream of traffic and simply stop for a while. The new federal highway system is particularly faulty in this respect. It not only has few such stopping places but no service areas at all! The parkways have more frequent and attractive service areas but they, too, lack enough rest areas and, of course, parking along them is otherwise completely prohibited except for "emergencies."

Local Traffic Problems

When confronted by a traffic problem, especially within towns and cities, the municipal officials usually call in a traffic engineer to help solve it. These professionals are expert in making traffic counts, origin and destination studies, and on staggering peak loads, alternate routing, and like remedial measures. They seldom show any interest in the effect their recommendations would have on the appearance and other amenities of the community; hence their recommendations should be carefully scrutinized before they are adopted so as to determine what the total effect will be.

Not all through traffic is of the heavy type, nor is all local traffic light. Truck deliveries to various commercial areas in a community must be made and many of these trucks are large and noisy. It is, therefore, desirable to keep them out of the residential districts as much as possible, and also to provide definite routes adequate for their use.

Street Widenings

No street widening should be undertaken without a careful study. To provide for the movement of more and more traffic vast programs of street widening have, from time to time, been carried out but these, at best, are mere palliative measures since the more you widen a street the greater is the traffic volume it encourages. Sooner or later the condition becomes just as bad as it was before the remedial measures were taken. Not only that but these widenings and straightenings cause all sorts of havoc.

Widenings must be considered not only from the point of

view of their effectiveness in respect to traffic movement but also their effect on the appearance and livability of the neighborhood. Many a good neighborhood has been ruined by the thoughtless widening of a street which encouraged heavy truck traffic to use it.

One of the things we have never been able to understand is why, when necessity demands the widening of a street on which fine trees exist, the authorities insist on cutting down all the trees and widening the road on both sides. Why can't they make a divided roadway, leaving all the trees on both sides of the old road, with the trees that were on one side now in a center mall? This sort of thing happens all the time and no one seems to be willing to organize effective protests. Sometimes it is a widening of an insignificant few feet to eliminate a slight narrowing of a highway for a block or so that is not really important from a traffic point of view but that may require the elimination of fine, old trees or the cutting off of front yards and perhaps front porches from houses on abutting land. It may involve cutting down miles of established trees and hedgerows along a country road. For whatever reason it is done, it is detrimental to community beauty and it ought to be stopped. Surely some other less destructive solution to the problem can be found.

For example, in connection with a new subdivision it is possible to construct service roads, only two car lanes wide, on each side of the original road which becomes a through lane with no curb parking permitted on it. This works well when the area is vacant farm or forest land. Builders fight it because it requires them to build two additional roadways along what they think of as an existing street. Such a solution is a good thing for the municipality, the neighborhood, and the motorist.

If a widening must be accomplished, it is foolish to take only a narrow strip of land. It is better to take plenty so that the reconstructed street can be built as a parked street with ample paved width both sides of a center mall in which street trees and other planting will have adequate room in which to develop properly. Measures of this sort are like the proverbial nettle—they must be firmly grasped if one is to avoid injury. If a street is going to have to be widened eventually, do it now, at once, and get it over with rather than taking a few feet now and more a few years hence. It will cost less in the long run and only one big upset will be required instead of a series of small, recurring ones.

Much of the blame for the deterioration of communities facing on or near through roads and express turnpikes must be laid at the door of the highway engineers. Nothing quite mars the original pattern of towns and cities and destroys their pleasant and agreeable situation as much as a very wide street or highway cutting through them. These should be given greater thought and care as to their alignment and location than has been their fortune in the past. Here is where the advice of the trained landscape architect and the architect can be utilized to great advantage. Such men are able to see space relationships in land and buildings and can visualize what the effect of a project will be without having to wait until it is completed. This ability, which is a part of their training, is ordinarily not possessed by the untrained layman, nor very often by members of the engineering profession.

Slow-moving local traffic, though it has its peaks, is not very heavy at any one time. It can be accommodated on relatively narrow streets with steeper grades and sharper curves. To establish uniform pavement widths throughout a neighborhood is probably inadvisable. Roadways should be designed for the amount of traffic they may be expected to carry.

Encouraging builders to lay out parklike streets is a long step toward civic beautification. Care in designing the planting areas and in choice of plant material to be used is, however, of utmost importance. Ample space must be provided for future growth, and the problems of curb parking (if permitted), snow removal (in the northern sections), and vandalism (everywhere) must be considered. Center malls, if they are to accommodate trees and shrubs must be more than 6 feet wide. Side areas between the edge of the roadway and the sidewalk, if any, or the property line must also be as wide as possible. A width of 50 feet has become an almost universally adopted standard width for residential streets. This provides for a 30-foot pavement and two 10-foot side areas which must also include sidewalks. If the pavement is narrowed to 22 feet, which is perfectly practicable on minor residential streets, and if curb parking is prohibited, the side strips can be increased to 14 feet which will accommodate street trees as well as a sidewalk. To provide for a center mall a right-of-way width of at least 70 feet is needed and 74 feet, or even more, is better. This provides for a 10-foot mall, two roadways each 22 feet wide and two 10-foot side strips including the sidewalks. Obviously considerably wider rights of way are desirable if it is possible to obtain them.

Pedestrian Traffic

The other type of traffic that often causes difficulties in a built-up community is pedestrian traffic. Too little thought has been given to this problem. It has been assumed that a narrow sidewalk bordering residential streets, or no sidewalk at all, is what is required; in business districts wider sidewalks have generally been provided but these are often rendered less efficient by placing parking meters, hydrants, sidewalk vaults, signs, street trees and, often, the overflow of merchandise from the stores themselves, within the sidewalk areas.

Some forward-looking municipalities are beginning to require that commercial buildings be set back at least ten feet from the building line. This permits retaining a narrow strip adjacent to the curb where all the meters, hydrants and so on can be placed where they will be out of the way of the sidewalk traffic. If curb parking is permitted, this area cannot be well maintained in turf or ground cover as it has to be crossed repeatedly; therefore Belgian block, brick, concrete "pavers," or gravel may be used, thereby reducing the amount of concrete and adding greatly to the appearance of the street. The provision of occasional seats or benches along the curb where shoppers can stop and rest is characteristic of some southern cities. This use of street furniture should be much encouraged elsewhere.

In trying to solve the street traffic problem some traffic experts and others have advocated narrowing the sidewalks, even in commercial and business districts, to less than the typical ten or fifteen feet. Nothing could be more detrimental to the orderly flow of pedestrian traffic. It would react badly on the adjacent businesses because most people like to window-shop and if sidewalks are narrow and they are continuously jostled by other pedestrians, the pleasure of this activity is reduced and possible customers lost.

It is important to separate pedestrian and vehicular traffic as much as possible. Where the two cannot be separated, as at street intersections, provisions must be made both for the safety of the pedestrian and for such easy and continuous flow of motor traffic as is concomitant with safety. Many devices have been invented and employed, some successful from the point of view of the pedestrian but frustrating to the motorist, others helpful to the motorist but terrifying to the pedestrian. A solution that seems fair from both points of view is yet to be found.

On wide streets traffic islands, which are supposed to be safe for pedestrians, are often installed, but unless these are fully protected by railings or stout abutments they may not be as safe as they are supposed to be. Where streets are wide enough to provide a real mall in the center to divide the two opposing lines of traffic, real safety is possible. It should be emphasized that pedestrian traffic control depends largely upon education. Police campaigns against jaywalking, instructions to children boarding and leaving school buses, and to motorists regarding these, are producing some beneficial results. Signs along the road warning of danger and noting speed limits may have some value, though, because there are so many of these, motorists tend to disregard them.

Old, uneven sidewalks in the older parts of our communities are a source of danger, especially to the elderly and infirm, and the combination of certain types of pavements or gratings and women's spiked heels are dangerous. Repair of these defective pedestrian ways will not only bring added safety but will improve the appearance of the area as well.

The question of whether or not to advocate the use of curbs along all highways in built-up areas is a moot one. No doubt curbs tend to define and protect the edge of the pavement but they also produce an effect of regimentation that, to these writers at least, is somewhat undesirable. If bituminous or Belgian block curbs are used instead of concrete, undesirable hardness of curb lines is made less evident.

The idea of arcaded sidewalks, or double-decked ones, has never caught on in this country to any extent. But these are very practical ideas and tend to enhance the beauty and interest of the community. People travel great distances to see the famous "rows" at Chester, England, which are nothing more than arcaded sidewalks, in two tiers, with shops on both levels. The arcades do darken the shops but with modern lighting this is not too great a drawback. The arcades are a shelter from the sun (rare in England) and from the rain (which is frequent).

In many Italian and French towns, and a few towns in our own South and Southwest where the Spanish influence is felt, arcaded streets and squares are frequent. In many of our larger towns and cities where narrow streets have become inadequate to handle the traffic volume, it should be possible to arcade the buildings, place the sidewalks within them, and do away with the present sidewalks, thus widening the street by at least two lanes. This would not require the condemnation of any property, merely the acquisition by the municipality of an easement for the arcaded sidewalks. The depth of the abutting ground-floor shops would be reduced by the width of the arcade but this would be a small price to pay for the added street width and the consequent easing of traffic flow, not to mention pedestrian and shopper comfort. The improvement in the appearance of our commercial districts would be immense.

6. Open Spaces Within the Community: Small Parks and Squares

The urban designer looks at the physical community as a combination of open and closed spaces. The closed spaces are the areas covered by buildings. The open spaces are the streets, yards, parking lots and, most importantly, the small squares, monument sites and parks, that can be treated in a decorative way. If properly designed and developed these can add a great deal to the beauty of the neighborhood in which they lie, and to the community as a whole. Many communities are justly famous for their public squares (Savannah), or for their plantings such as the azalea trail, an extended parklike treatment along the main highways in Norfolk, Virginia, and Mobile, Alabama; the dogwood plantings in many places such as on Greenfield Hill, Fairfield, Connecticut; the rose gardens at Charlotte, North Carolina, and Portland, Oregon; and the many quiet commons that grace so many New England towns and villages.

People are quick to recognize the opportunities for civic beautification in some such site and are quite concerned when they see that an area that has potentialities for great beauty is either not being well maintained, has been poorly laid out and developed, or is being neglected entirely. They realize that something ought to be done about this situation and a great deal of community interest can be aroused by an active club or committee that decides to undertake a project of development or rehabilitation for some such place.

Danger exists, of course, that more steam than common sense will be generated and time and money are often spent fruitlessly on projects that should never have been started in the first place, or that were not properly organized. Enthusiasm alone is not sufficient. An appalling number of these small ill-advised projects are undertaken every year. Most of this amateur design is shockingly bad. Much of the resulting work, which turns out usually to be planting of one sort or another, is poorly designed and hence, in a short time, becomes more of a liability than an asset. Good basic design in all of these projects is of paramount importance. Without it they are futile. Planting, while important too, should carry out the basic design and never attempt to hide its lack. Projects of this sort generally need professional guidance and, before anything is done, this should be obtained. A competent landscape architect or an architect can show an interested group how to go about a project of this sort, and his advice will save a great deal of time and money. His modest fee will be money well spent.

There are several sorts of these open spaces, each with its own peculiar characteristics. Any proper program for design, redesign, or rehabilitation will, therefore, have to suit the particular area being dealt with. One would not treat a simple village common in the same manner as one would a downtown, formal square in a commercial area, nor small open spaces at street intersections in the same way as a rocky ravine or hillside.

Small Areas at Street Intersections

A group of typical small areas having similar characteristics are those that often occur at street intersections, around bus stops, conveniences, and public buildings on relatively small sites. These areas may be treated in a purely decorative manner and can be made most attractive. Trees and shrubs, carefully selected and arranged so that they do not interfere with the clear vision of traffic, and even flowers and ground covers can be used to increase the beauty of such areas. Generally the question of easy maintenance should be kept in mind, but if the services of a competent caretaker are available quite a lot more can be done than is usually considered possible.

Travelers exclaim over the way these small, almost inconsequential, areas are treated in Europe. Every little space is planted with something, either flowering shrubs as in England, bulbs followed by annuals in the Netherlands, bedding plants meticulously constrained to fit some intricate design as in France, or exuberant beds of colorful annuals in Italy. Why can't it be done here? Mainly because nobody takes enough interest to see that such places are well planted and well cared for. We recall, years ago, when railroads employed grade-crossing watchmen, that around many of their little shelters colorful gardens were maintained. Most of these men were immigrants trained in the European tradition. Growing flowers and vegetables in their spare time came naturally to them.

Nowhere is the difference in attitude between the United States and Europe shown more plainly than in the care and treatment of the land around a gas station. In this country such facilities, necessary though they are, are generally eyesores. In Europe the areas around such stations, which in themselves are well designed and attractive, are beautifully maintained and often extremely well planted.

Planting, however, is not the only thing that can be done to improve these small, open areas. Paving can be laid and low walls and steps can be built. A wide variety of paving materials and colored gravels are available and their judicious use can add a great deal of interest to what might otherwise be a rather dull area. These materials, if well laid, are much easier and cheaper to maintain than either turf or ground covers, and in many ways are more practical especially for an area that is not used but is mainly to look at. Good design is more important than anything else because line, pattern, balance, and proportion can create interest independently of plant material. Most such areas are more effective if developed quite simply, not overplanted or overdecorated. Highly detailed and fussy arrangements are inappropriate. It often takes the judgment of a trained landscape architect or architect to decide what to do, how much, and what to omit. Of course nothing should be done that will now or later on interfere with traffic, nor provide dark areas that are difficult to supervise.

Although in designing such areas simplicity should be the rule there is no reason why, if the money to install and maintain them is available, seasonal floral displays cannot be arranged for. Tulips in the spring, geraniums, petunias, or begonias in the summer, and chrysanthemums in the fall can be successfully used in such places in many sections of the country. They are colorful and do not require a great deal of care. Other plants can be used in other regions, such as succulents in the Southwest, azaleas in the deep South and so on.

Downtown Parks and Squares

In the larger squares or small parks either in the downtown core area of the community or in outlying residential areas, much greater freedom of treatment is possible and desirable. These are areas that people will walk through or into and possibly remain in for a time, whereas the areas just discussed are seldom entered by anyone except maintenance personnel and are viewed from outside.

If these small parks and squares are made attractive and inviting, many people will use them. Main walks should therefore be wider than normal sidewalks, say ten to twelve feet instead of the usual four to six. They should be laid out not so much to follow an arbitrary pattern, however attractive that might be, but to follow the directions people will normally take to cross the area. In this way corner cutting will be minimized and the maintenance problem reduced. When faced with the problem of designing the path system for such an area the temptation is strong to devise an interesting, abstract pattern and then impose it on the area. This may possibly produce an attractive plan on paper but it will not necessarily produce a workable design. One should first study the area, its surroundings, approaches, and the way people may be expected to use it and then evolve the design around these use patterns.

Such parks and squares should be adequately and attractively furnished. Plenty of permanent, comfortable and well-designed benches should be provided, but also enough portable chairs so that people can gather in small groups for conversation or game playing. Of course some of these chairs will disappear in time, but that is a small price to pay for more pleasurable use of the area that they make possible. In the Tuileries Gardens in Paris an old woman comes along from time to time to collect the wandering chairs and returns them to their proper place, collecting en route a few sous from other occupants. Would we could install a similar system here! Well-placed and attractive trash bins should also be provided and, if possible, drinking fountains. Where the use of the area is likely to be extremely heavy, lawn areas should be reduced and interesting and varied pavements substituted for them. Flagpoles and a modicum of sculpture or possibly a fountain can also be appropriately used in such places.

Maintenance is still a paramount consideration and nothing should be planted or built that will be so difficult to take care of that it will prove impossible to keep in good condition. These small parks and squares should never be treated as "bosky dells." The temptation to overplant these areas is terrific, but it should be firmly resisted. As these areas are generally surrounded by streets and buildings, a formal treatment is more suitable than a naturalistic one unless the topography strongly dictates otherwise. Naturalistic treatments that call for winding pathways and heavy planting often create too many police problems. It should always be possible to see into and across the area from any vantage point outside. This means that dense, enclosing shrub borders creating dark nooks and crannies are probably ruled out entirely unless the whole park or square is brilliantly lighted at night or securely closed after dark.

The design treatment depends somewhat on the character of the neighborhood in which the small park is located. If it is in a run-down area frequented by idlers and undesirables, it must remain so open that hiding places within it are minimized. At the same time it must contain enough greenery to have a desirable influence on the neighborhood around it. If it is in a much better residential or commercial neighborhood it can be treated more freely and lavishly.

European cities seem to have less trouble with this problem of crime and vandalism than American cities do. Hyde Park, Green Park, and St. James's in London, the Tuileries in Paris and the Royal Park in Athens, are open at all times, and not particularly well lighted, but no serious police problems except to a limited extent in London seem to have developed. In this country, however, we often have serious problems. Central Park and Morningside Park in New York City, and parks in other places, have become notoriously unsafe.

Most of our older communities already have a certain number of these downtown, open spaces. Most of them, however, seem to need redesign and rehabilitation. Where spaces are lacking, efforts should be made to provide them.

This can often be done in connection with some urban renewal project or a large, private commercial or industrial development. To be properly useful they should be located where both shoppers and workers will find them convenient to use. In good weather shoppers can stop to rest awhile and workers can eat their lunches there. The churchyards of Trinity and St. Paul's in lower New York City have served this purpose for years for countless office workers. If such an attractive place is provided, the tired shopper will rest there awhile and then return to shop some more rather than going home, which will help business.

Parklets

Small areas, frequently referred to as parklets, can often be created where some old, obsolete building has been torn down. Usually such spaces become parking lots but it would often be much wiser to make them into parklets for people to use and admire. This is quite simple and inexpensive to do. The area can be paved in an interesting pattern with a variety of materials combining concrete, brick, flagstone, and gravel. A few areas can be left unpaved to be filled with suitable low plants and perhaps a small tree or two. Evergreens or vines can be planted against the adjoining buildings to soften their bare ugliness. Sometimes a small, pleasing wall fountain can be introduced to add variety, interest, and the sound of dripping water. A particularly lovely little green oasis of this sort has been created between two tall buildings on Chestnut Street in Philadelphia. Plenty of comfortable benches, a milk, coffee, or soft-drink dispensing machine help make these areas more usable. Suitable night lighting will make them attractive in the evening hours. If necessary they can be fenced so as to make locking them at night a possibility, but if they are properly designed this would rarely be necessary.

Because many downtown open areas have become hang-outs for the teen-age groups on mischief bent, or derelicts of one sort or another, many people have been reluctant to spend much time and thought on the rehabilitation of down-town open spaces. But as they are so important to civic development and beautification they should by no means remain neglected. Through zoning, and other promotional means those enterprises that will attract evening crowds can be induced to locate in the downtown commercial area making it a center of evening activity instead of allowing it to remain a dead spot.

We repeat and stress again the importance of good design in all these parks and related areas. The pattern itself should show good scale and proportion, the planting should be carefully chosen not only for durability but also for interesting form, color, and texture. Paving material should be interesting and structures should be designed by a competent architect. If they are well done they can add immensely to the attractiveness of the area. If they are merely utilitarian they contribute dullness where brightness is required, and if they are ugly they can ruin the whole effect. No one of these attributes should take precedence over the others. The object is to produce a unified whole. This cannot be done if the matter is approached, as it often is, as a "project to plant the park." Planting is important but it is only one among several equally important considerations. Garden-club groups are particularly vulnerable to this approach. They often tend to think in terms of planting and horticulture rather than in terms of complete design.

Monuments

The use of small open spaces such as squares and parks as sites for public monuments is a well-established custom. It would seem, unfortunately, that not all, nor even a majority, of these monuments have been well placed. We all are familiar with the ubiquitous Civil-War soldier on his pedestal in the town square. Many of these today have become traffic hazards owing to improper location in the first place or the slow but sure nibbling away of the land around them by street widenings.

Many honor rolls were hastily erected after both the First and the Second World War. Some of these have been replaced by permanent memorials but many have not and often present a delapidated appearance. Some were backed up with planting which was small and attractive when put in place but now, after forty years or so, has grown all out of scale or has become ragged and disreputable. If, as often happens, a war memorial is located in a park or public square, ample space must be provided around it to accommodate large numbers of people who, on ceremonial occasions, will gather at such a place, and as a result any planting in the area is likely to be trampled on. Even lawns will suffer. Probably much of such an area should be graveled or paved, but this can be done in an interesting manner if the materials are carefully selected and laid.

If monuments to commemorate an event or to honor an individual, and their surrounding architectural elements like paved areas, steps, and seats are well sited and designed, they can become the focal point of an entire park scheme. They always should seem integrated into the complete design, not appear as though they were an afterthought. If one monument constitutes a focal point, then other monuments in the same square or small park must be subsidiary to it or banned entirely. Competition among such features is to be avoided.

When monuments and historical markers are placed near roadsides they, too, should be provided with ample space in front of them so that motorists can pull out of the traffic, stop, and get out. This is particularly true where the inscription is long or where the lettering is small. There is little use in putting up such monuments and markers if no one dares to stop to read them because no place to do this safely has been provided.

Badly placed and neglected monuments, honor rolls, and historic markers offer an opportunity for civic beautification that need not wait on larger considerations. These are immediate problems that can be dealt with on an individual basis. Of course, before doing much or spending money, it is wise to find out whether the municipal officials have any plans that would permanently affect the sites of these features. If they lie within a street widening area, or an area to be taken over for some other purpose, or if they stand on privately owned land it is well to find out about this before proceeding.

Usually no such problem arises and a group, club, or committee can safely start to raise funds for the rehabilitation, redesign, or relocation of this important feature. Sometimes it is necessary or advisable to move one of these back from the highway to take it out of the line of vision of motorists. Many times these features need a proper background planting or a paved foreground area. They should not, however, be overplanted or surrounded with wide flower beds so that it is impossible to get near enough to read the inscriptions.

Maintenance of these monuments and similar features is of great importance. Birds are all very well and probably should be encouraged to frequent these small parks and squares but birds, particularly pigeons, are dirty. Nothing is so indicative of poor municipal housekeeping as a statue or monument covered with bird droppings. The same thing is true of public buildings. Traffic-worn turf tends to downgrade the appearance of a public square or small park. Therefore the area around most monuments and honor rolls which attract a great deal of traffic should be paved.

In fact the general maintenance of these open spaces is

important if they are to remain attractive spots. We have stressed easy and low-cost maintenance for all public open spaces because many park and highway departments fear inroads on their budgets, especially in small communities. They therefore hesitate to give consent to plans for rehabilitation or development of such areas. It is mandatory, therefore, that before any such project is undertaken, a clear and amicable understanding is arrived at with the people who are going to have to maintain the work when completed. It is useless to fix up a park, square, or monument site, or pay for the construction of some shelter or other building in connection with such a place, if the municipal authorities are going to be unwilling to include sufficient funds for maintenance in their budget, or if the actual people who are going to do the work do not know how or do not care.

We refer particularly to the awful treatment often meted out to shrubs planted in such public park areas. The ignorance of the average highway or park superintendent as to how to care for these plants is appalling. More good plant material has been butchered than one would care to contemplate. Shearing shrubs back year after year until they are nothing but shrubby bunches of twigs unable to bear a flower does not improve community appearance. By proper pruning, shrubs can be held in check for years without ruining their appearance. If and when they get out of scale or out of hand and are much too big for their locations, they should be removed and be replaced with new and slower-growing material. No planting, regardless of how carefully the plants have been selected, is permanent. Plants grow! Perhaps it is incumbent upon the various garden clubs to supervise pruning or to see that at least a minimum amount of instruction is given on this important phase of civic beautification.

Pedestrian Malls

So-called pedestrian malls, either roofed over or open to the sky, in downtown commercial areas have recently aroused a great deal of interest as a means of reviving and making older core areas more attractive. Some have been tried and found successful, others, for one reason or another, have failed. Where successful, people have returned to their former habits of shopping downtown instead of rushing off to the outlying areas where shopping centers have sprung up with adequate parking facilities.

The usual approach to the creation of such a mall is to close off some block or street against motor traffic, to devote the area to wide pedestrian walkways and to embellish with trees, shrubs, water features, and beds of flowers. To do this it is not always necessary to tear up the existing pavement as most plantings can be done in raised plant boxes of wood or masonry. This is an excellent way to do if the outcome of the experiment is in doubt. If it fails, all this decoration can easily be removed and the area restored to its former use at low cost. If and when the experiment becomes a proven success it is usually wise to plant the trees permanently in spaces cut into the paving and filled with good soil, or in larger properly prepared planting areas.

In general, especially if the mall is covered with glass or plastic, the planting has to be considered purely as stage scenery and not as permanent, growing material. Plants do not survive for long under these artificial conditions and frequent renewal is almost always necessary. A program for replacement, succession of special floral features and the like, should be worked out in advance and funds made available either through the municipality or through an association of the merchants in the area. Many of these downtown shopping malls have been made very attractive with their gay plantings, their lively fountains, and benches carefully placed to make them a boon to tired shoppers.

To be successful, however, a downtown shopping and pedestrian mall needs more than attractive planting, water features, and the like. It must be backed by an adequate and convenient parking area and by adequate highways or public transportation to enable people to get there. The problem has to be tackled simultaneously from all angles, not just from the aspect of civic beautification, which is a most necessary and appealing one to be sure, but not the only one. Statistics and surveys show that well-designed and well-decorated pedestrian malls with sufficient nearby parking space and easy access do increase business and greatly improve the appearance of the community. The mere removal of through traffic from a downtown retail area will work wonders and if, after this is done by providing a proper system of ring roads around the central core, the area is revivified by adequate planting, a good mall design, and street furniture, business can be brought back to it.

Street Decoration

Other things, perhaps less drastic than the creation of a pedestrian mall in the downtown area, can be done to liven up and beautify the community. Most commercial areas originally had street trees, often magnificent ones. In the name of progress many of these were ruthlessly destroyed. Others, like the American elm and chestnut, succumbed or are succumbing to disease. Still others could not survive adverse conditions caused by too much pavement, too many overhead wires, and just plain old age. They should have been replaced. Nothing adds so much charm to a shopping street as well-cared-for trees. They soften the appearance of the architecture, which is often undistinguished and inharmonious, they provide shade during hot weather, they help dispel an undesirable citified atmosphere. Choosing the right sort of tree is, however, of the utmost importance. They should have high branches, not too wide spread, and be able to withstand the trying conditions of heat, drought, and gasoline fumes.

In some towns well-planted flower baskets are hung from the street lighting standards but unless these are well maintained they fail to continue to be attractive. In several towns where these baskets have been put in place the local fire department, as its contribution to civic beautification, comes along at regular intervals and waters them from a hose wagon so that they remain bright and flourishing. The local florists keep watch of the project, too, and make the necessary replacements and changes.

Where space permits, concrete or wooden planters can be placed along the edges of the sidewalk or in a center mall in a wide street and these can be filled with a series of seasonal displays starting with bulbs in the spring and ending with Christmas trees in December. Pittsfield, Massachusetts, has used rowan trees (mountain ash) in planters along its Main Street to good effect. New York City uses large concrete containers along Fifth Avenue and Park Avenue South. In many places the merchants use planters and potted material to help bring a touch of color and interest to the shopping district. People will throw trash into such planters and pots but its removal is merely one of those necessary chores that are a part of good municipal housekeeping.

Of course the whole business of Christmas decoration comes under the head of civic beautification but as it is temporary it need not concern us at length here. But be it said that strings of multicolored lights are not always an added attraction and that the bellowing of carols from loudspeakers for weeks before the day itself is not always pleasant nor does it attract customers.

Landscape Development for Public Buildings

Another place people quickly recognize as an opportunity for civic beautification is around such public buildings as the library, town hall, police station, courthouse, railroad station, or other prominently located public buildings. If the appearance of these is improved the whole community benefits. Overenthusiastic engagement in such projects, however, presents dangers. Overplanting and a profusion of inappropriate and fussy details may result.

If such a building stands in a large square or small park, as often happens, the treatment around it must be an integral part of the design of the whole area—it must blend harmoniously with it and not appear as something apart and different from its surroundings. Why is it that in contemporary America we seem to feel that every important building should rise from a billowing mass of foliage, preferably evergreen? No Italian villa, French château, or English manor house, the prototypes of many of our public buildings of former years, is so burdened. These may have their gardens and plantations, but at a distance, not crowded against the building itself. Modern buildings also resent this treatment. Shrub and tree groups should be arranged to enframe the building or to create a background. The plantings should embellish not obliterate. Our approach probably stems from the great attention given to contemporary private residences where a rich foundation planting has become a highly regarded status symbol. This is a peculiarly American phenomenon, rarely met with elsewhere.

The landscape treatment of any public building should have a dignity commensurate with the building it embellishes. A carefully thought-out design is imperative. The paths, walks, and driveways must be of ample width and properly placed for convenience and easy access. At entrances, which will normally be wide enough to carry the expected amount of traffic without having to worry about crowding, adequate paved space must be provided where people may congregate. The walkways should be so designed that corner-cutting will be minimized and ugly curbs or railings will not have to be erected to protect the lawn areas. The device of planting groups of shrubs at such locations should not have to be resorted to.

The principle of proper scale is most important in any planting intended to embellish a building. If it is large, as many such structures are, planting small shrubs or flowering plants near it is ineffective and inappropriate. Large building masses demand large plants and usually not many of them and plenty of open areas to provide an adequate setting. All plants should be arranged as groups designed to create pictorial compositions rather than being mere plant collections strung along the building facade. Main entrances may be accentuated by matched pairs of exceptionally fine plants, preferably evergreen for year round effect. It should be remembered that simplicity and restraint are of cardinal importance. It is far better to use a few plants of sufficient size than to set out a clutter of small plants, either scattered over the entire area or crowded into beds here and there, that have little or no significance in the design. Floral display of herbaceous material should be placed at a distance from the building itself and should only be considered when the maintenance can be expected to be of a high order.

Parking facilities for those who work in the building must be provided for and also for a reasonable number of visitors. It is most annoying when trying to do business with a public agency to have to park blocks away. To create adequate parking, however, the character of the area surrounding the building should not be jeopardized. Lawn areas should not be encroached upon for this purpose or fine trees cut down, as often happens. If the site lacks room for proper parking a parking lot should be arranged for nearby but off the site.

Landscape Development of School Grounds

The little red school house (seldom was it red, they say) is a thing of the past, and today enormous, sprawling structures are springing up all over the country to house the educational program for our children. These buildings contain the very latest in equipment for teaching all sorts of things but very little is usually done about the grounds around the buildings except to lay the necessary walks and driveways, a ball field, running track, and usually inadequate parking space. Often the matter of site development is included in the architect's contract though he may not know a great deal about landscape development; he may, therefore, call in a landscape contractor or nurseryman to plant a few trees and bushes here and there to "landscape" the property. Furthermore, the school board frequently finds that the building is costing much more than it was thought it would, and so takes whatever small amounts of money that may have been earmarked for grounds development to help finish the building. The result is that the planting and the general grounds development is shockingly bad.

It should be mandatory that when a school project is started the architect and the landscape architect be commissioned simultaneously, and that a proper proportion of the funds be allotted to each for his part of the project with no possibility that either could borrow from the other to make up shortages that may occur. In this way we would get a much more satisfactory solution to the problem. If we go on as we are we never will.

A properly designed and developed school site can become a highly regarded focal point in the community. Time was when the largest and most important looking building in town was the school. Modern school buildings lack this imposing character, but if the grounds about such buildings are well developed the whole composition can become important enough to warrant pointing to it with pride. Educators seem not to realize the educational influence of architectural and landscape-architectural design on young minds. If children are exposed to beauty at an impressionable age, they will absorb it unconsciously and develop discriminating taste in later years. We try to teach them art appreciation, music appreciation, and the like. Why not architectural and landscape appreciation? And where better to display good examples than on the school grounds?

School sites today are ample in size. Much of the area is used for organized games and quite properly so, but there is always a lot of land left over that could be used to create a more beautiful setting for the building and much that could be developed into a more parklike composition. It is much easier today to get money to buy a large school site than to buy land for a much-needed park. We are convinced that our children must be educated but we do not seem at all sure that a park is necessary. Why not, then, combine the two?

If around our school buildings we use trees to enframe the architectural mass, or in groups at a distance to hide objectionable views, or to provide a grove to create a shady area for outdoor classes, or if we use generous shrub and evergreen borders to serve as sight and sound barriers to protect neighborhood residences from school activities and to create a real composition of building, open areas, and planting—in other words a real landscape, not a contrived one—we will really have accomplished something. Such a development would be the pride of the community possessing it, an attractive oasis of greenery in any urban setting.

With all the land around our contemporary school buildings it is truly remarkable that practically none of it is developed or used for genuine outdoor educational purposes. Of course athletics and other types of physical education are often taught outdoors though they can be, and often are, taught indoors. The basic principles of botany, geology, and zoology can, however, be taught outdoors much more effectively than in the classroom. Under the guidance of the late L. B. Sharp the Outdoor Education Association, in cooperation with a number of schools and universities, has developed and operated a comprehensive program of outdoor education. Much of this is conducted in camps located in wilderness situations but much of it can be carried out on the home school grounds or college campus if the faculties of these institutions would but realize the possibilities and the opportunities for a broader, more realistic educational program that they are missing. "Land for learning," a phrase coined by Dr. Sharp, expresses the whole philosophy of learning in the outdoors. Let the land around our school buildings be so developed that it can be devoted to real learning and not entirely to recreation and embellishment.

7. Open Spaces for Recreation

In recent years the subject of public recreation has received a great deal more attention than it did in the past. This is partly because of the shorter work week which makes available to many more people much more leisure than they formerly enjoyed, and partly because as communities continue to build up, vacant lots and other open spaces for free play disappear. Parents realize that if children are to develop into well-rounded personalities they must have safe, well-equipped play areas.

It is not nearly so difficult to arouse enthusiasm for a program to promote recreation as it is to stir up the same degree of excitement for simple civic beautification. It is, therefore, often expedient to combine the two objectives. And why not? There is no reason why recreation areas should not be attractive as well as useful. Children's playgrounds do not have to be nothing more than fenced-in concrete platforms, ball-field grandstands need not be ugly, though they usually are, and all sorts of recreation facilities, from the simplest to the most elaborate, can just as easily as not be made more attractive and add to civic beauty.

In devising recreation areas it has been found wise to separate those who are to use the facilities into various age groups, beginning with the tiny tots, up to the age of six or so, who require their own particular type of play space, progressing through the older elementary school children who need more space and a somewhat different program, to the teen-age group who not only need even more space but have reached the age when they do not require so much supervision and can invent some of their own activities, and finally reaching the young adult, the older adult, and even the elderly groups who all require recreational activities suited to their needs and desires.

Projects to serve the recreational activities of these various groups which will at the same time improve the appearance of the community can be developed in nearly every small town or city and in many suburban communities where open space is becoming scarce. In fact larger communities may need many such areas. Existing facilities, to fully realize their potential, may also need to be redesigned and rehabilitated. New ones should, of course, be laid out with appearance as well as utility in mind. The citizens of the neighborhood in which such a recreational facility is to be located should see that this is done.

Specialists in the field of recreation and sport tend to concentrate their attention on the physical requirements of various activities. Ball fields and tennis courts must be level, of a certain size and properly oriented. Other activities make similar demands. In locating them these may not be disregarded and the task of the designer becomes a problem in meeting these requirements and, at the same time, coming up with a design that possesses aesthetic qualities as well. It is, therefore, wise to arrange that the recreation specialists consult with a qualified landscape architect whenever any recreational area project is being planned.

Tot-lots

The very name of these areas indicates that they are of limited size and intended for the use of very young children,

probably below the age of six, who will be under the supervision of mothers or nursemaids. According to statistics com-
piled by the Westchester County (N.Y.) Planning Department, these tot-lots should be from 1500 to 5000 square feet
in size and should be designed to provide 50 square feet of
play space per child. They should be located at frequent
enough intervals in the community so that no child would
have to walk more than a short distance to reach one and, of
course, they should be located so that children will not have
to cross unprotected main traffic arteries.

These lots should contain a certain amount of play equipment, play sculpture as it is often called, a sandbox, and comfortable benches or chairs for the mothers or nursemaids who
will be present to supervise the children's play. Whenever
possible this sitting area should be at least partially shaded
by a tree or a shelter of some sort. The play area should be
large enough so that the enclosing fence can be hidden, or at
least disguised by shrubbery or hedges. These are the basic
minimums. How much more can be provided to make these
play areas more attractive is up to the sponsors, who may be
a private housing developer, the municipality, a service club,
or the neighborhood families using the place. All too often
tot-lots are nothing more than a fenced rectangle of concrete
with a few bits and pieces of equipment scattered about.
They lack shade, they lack places where children can dig or
use their imagination in any way. Young children often find
such places boring and, when inside the fence, they often
feel imprisoned and want out.

This latter sort of play space is found not only in "high-
rise" slum-clearance projects in metropolitan areas where
they seem ubiquitous, but also in connection with suburban
and village "garden-apartment" developments. Zoning ordinances generally require that such projects cover only fifty
to sixty per cent of the area with structures. The remaining
land is available for parking spaces, driveways, walks, lawns

and planting spaces, and play space. The play space usually occupies a very small fraction of the area. These spaces ought to be enlarged so as to make them more useful and attractive. Open space and lawn areas are all very well but they add little to the enjoyment of life in these developments. As matters usually stand the children are getting the short end of the deal.

The whole idea of garden apartments and limited land coverage by buildings would seem to be to provide space on the ground and outdoors for human activities. Devoting most of this space to lawns which cannot be used but merely looked at defeats this purpose. We believe that in all such projects much more use should be made of the land. This would tend to populate it and reduce the problems of vandalism and crime that have become troublesome in many of these developments in cities and suburbs as well.

All these things apply not only to play spaces built in connection with an apartment-house development but to those established elsewhere and operated by the municipality. The need for these small play areas in the older parts of even small towns and villages is rather acute. These communities were built before the need for such facilities was clearly recognized and so they were not provided. But now the need is known and they should be created where they will best serve their proper purpose. The site where an obsolete building is torn down or a vacant lot in an established neighborhood are ideal spots.

Playgrounds for Older Children

Playgrounds are defined by authorities on recreation as local facilities providing a wide range of activities for the group of children older than the tiny tots, but younger than the young teen-agers. It is traditionally a place for active play for elementary school children, but since most modern schools, especially in small towns and suburbs, have well equipped play areas of their own the separate neighborhood playground has broadened its field of activity to include more space and equipment, to widen the age group served, and to include some passive recreation pursuits.

Before embarking on a project to promote the establishment of a neighborhood playground, or for the redesign and rehabilitation of an existing, inadequate one, a survey of the area should be made to determine the needs and the desires of the people in and around the area. This should indicate how many people or families it is proposed to serve, the ages of the children to be considered and the type of activities that interest them. Children of this age group can no longer roam the neighborhood seeking places to play. They not only annoy the neighbors when they do this, but they also often get into trouble. Even in rather sparsely developed suburban neighborhoods open woodlands, ponds, and streams available to youngsters no longer exist. A playground equipped for constructive play without the possibility of destruction or disturbance to the neighborhood homes is needed.

Swings, seesaws, slides, and the like, but also areas for informal softball, basketball, handball and volleyball games should, therefore, be provided. There should be an open area for casual or free play. A wading pool is desirable and plenty of benches and tables in a quiet, shady location for the more quiet games and for arts and crafts. Professional advice both from a landscape architect and an architect should be obtained and the Playground Association of America, as well as the National Recreation Association, can provide valuable help in suggesting the needs of this group of youngsters. Any money spent on professional services of this sort will prove to be a wise investment. The object should be to make the playground useful and attractive and not merely dressed up. Good design will consider both use and beauty.

These playgrounds, when not attached to a school plant, can be established by the municipality, a service organization, or a group or association within the affected neighborhood. In either case adequate financing is imperative. Provision for the necessary maintenance and supervision must be made in advance. No project should be started until either the actual funds are in hand or reliable pledges or promises have been obtained for its forthcoming in the future when needed. The maintenance charges should be a community responsibility paid for out of tax revenues.

These areas should be from three to five acres in size. A five-acre playground has been estimated to be adequate for a population of 5000 but not for many more. Such a playground should, of course, be within easy walking distance of the children who will use it. It has been suggested that in a dense residential area this distance should not be much over one fourth of a mile, but this can be stretched to a half mile in more open developments.

Most efforts towards beautification of these playgrounds will be centered around suitable screen plantations, either shrubbery where there is enough room for it, or well-tended hedges. Trees are necessary to provide shade for the quiet areas and sometimes to screen out tall buildings in the vicinity, or ugly views. Flowers are probably seldom appropriate unless it should happen that someone in the sponsoring group is particularly interested in arousing children's interest in gardening, in which case a small area might be set aside for this activity. We believe, however, that herbaceous material should appear in such a place only for educational reasons, not for decoration as such. The design of fences, walls, pavements, and all structures is of great importance. They will set the keynote for the area but to be effective they need be neither elaborate nor expensive, but must be sturdily built and pleasing in appearance.

Playfields

Larger playgrounds or, as they are more commonly called, playfields for the use of the early teen-age groups offer more freedom in design as well as use. This group, ranging from nine or ten to fourteen, is old enough for organized games and space for these must be provided. Places for more imaginative play are most important. There should be trees to climb, places to dig and to permit opportunities to build, and, if by some good fortune, the site is rocky or has a stream running through it, the possibilities for free, inventive projects are almost limitless. Here, too, the less active or passive recreational activities must be provided for.

Although no attempt should be made to treat such playfields as decorative parks, they can certainly be made attractive as well as useful. We have observed many small town and village playfields of this type which have been developed without adequate planning. A baseball diamond is dropped here, perhaps sponsored by a local service club or a merchants' association interested in furthering the "Little League," or another feature is set down somewhere else, without regard to the rest of the area. Parking facilities are badly placed or entirely lacking, conveniences have not been provided, there are no drinking fountains, no shade, no fencing or other types of enclosure. The whole thing is uninviting and can actually become a community nuisance and eyesore rather than an asset.

These playfields are generally located in what are primarily residential neighborhoods, and properly so, but because they produce noise and commotion and, if they are lighted at night as they sometimes are, they can be a disturbing influence. They need to be designed and constructed with the greatest care to lessen these objections. In the first place the area should be large enough, two to ten acres, so that it can accommodate not only the proposed recreational activities but provide space for a generous screen plantation all around it. This does not mean a six-foot strip planted with a row of arborvitae or Norway spruce, as it often turns out to be. Rather, the enclosing plantation should be composed of trees and dense growing shrubs and be at least twenty-five feet in width, and preferably fifty. Without this depth of planting, noise and lights cannot be adequately screened off from the surrounding neighborhood. These planting screens, if well designed, can be objects of great beauty in themselves and add immensely to the attractiveness of the neighborhood.

For a playfield of this size and importance, professional advice should be obtained and the prepared plans adhered to. It often happens that funds to carry out the whole project are not immediately available. The temptation then is to substitute a cheap, temporary solution for the long-range development. Temporary things, however, have a way of becoming permanent and too often they prevent the original scheme from being properly carried out at a later date. It is better to start with a small section of the development with the funds in hand, but in accordance with the adopted design, and then take the next step when more funds are available.

Supervision of both playgrounds and playfields is imperative. Under the direction of the physical-education department of a nearby school, the Y.M.C.A., or a paid director who will run these play areas in the manner of a day camp, this problem can be solved. Sometimes the cost of this supervision can be included in the municipal budget, for most towns have the right to make such expenditures, or it might be included in the school district budget. In other instances such playgrounds and playfields have been sponsored and built by various service clubs or merchants' associations.

Teen-age and Adult Recreation Areas

When we begin to consider the needs of the upper teen-age and young adult groups in the community, play areas begin to take on the characteristics of parks. Their proper use includes not only organized games and associated activities but a large number of things that, because of the large amount of space they require, cannot be accommodated in the ordinary playfield embracing only a few acres. Both active and passive recreational purposes have to be considered but these areas require less close supervision.

Such park-playgrounds will provide regulation-sized baseball fields, a football field, and running tracks with their attendant and necessary "bleachers" or grandstands and probably a field house of some sort. Cycling and horseback riding may be possible. Skating, sliding, and even a small ski area can often be included. Recently swimming pools have become a very popular facility for this and for the older adult groups.

All these activities are of the more active sort. On the passive side facilities must be provided where people can stroll through pleasant surroundings, watch birds, walk their dogs, gather in groups for quiet games, or simply sit and read. People must be able to do these things without interruption from the more active groups. This means that the areas must be quite large and well planned to separate the various sorts of activities to their common advantage.

In the days when most people lived in small towns and villages, or even on farms, plenty of woodlands or vacant fields were available for games, picnics, and other family outings. Nowadays, when most people live in cities or suburbs, these open areas within a practical distance of our homes are fast disappearing. The need for parks and open spaces which can be used, even in our fairly low-density suburbs, is acute. This may, at first glance, seem odd since in these areas there appears to be some open space, even patches of undisturbed woodland. But none of this land is available for free use. It is all privately owned and trespassers are not tolerated. Many people who have moved to the suburbs so that their children would have room to roam are now finding that expansion and development have caught up with them and they are almost right back where they started. It has been fairly well established that the delinquency rate increases as the distance from a playground or park increases. Parks cannot cure delinquency but they can help mightily. Suburban residents should, therefore, be anxious to initiate and support a more intensive program for the acquisition and development of suburban park land.

Still another playing area that is becoming more and more popular is the golf course. These might be termed a cross between a playfield and a park. Public golf courses are being established more and more frequently in progressive communities. The cost of membership in private golf and country clubs makes it impossible for many people of moderate means to enjoy this activity. State parks partly fill this gap but they are generally inadequate to meet the need, especially if they are relatively near a large city. Privately operated golf courses, where play is paid for by greens fees, are also useful and popular but for many even these are too costly. Municipally operated golf links seem to be the best solution for the problem and often these can be developed in connection with the park-playgrounds already mentioned.

Large Parks and Reservations

Before it is too late every community should acquire as much open space as possible. Whenever feasible adult recreation areas, for example, can be extended and developed as a larger park thus affording the citizens greater opportunities for outdoor living and recreation, both active and passive. For when there is space enough these areas can contain, besides the usual recreational facilities, many more decorative and educational features like rose gardens and even a zoo.

The development of such large parks means a great deal to civic development and beautification but their design and development is beyond the ability of nonprofessional groups or organizations. The citizen's function in projects of this sort is to instigate and through education to build up an enthusiastic demand on the part of the community for such a thing. The ordinary citizen cannot be expected to do the actual designing or have control over it. He should, however, be aware of the purposes and possibilities of such a project, of the features which should be incorporated in it and those which should be rigorously ruled out. Then, when proposals to include something inappropriate, or to omit something essential, are made he can make effective protest at the proper time and in the right place.

The design of large parks is entirely within the province of the landscape architect who has been trained to develop large areas of land for use and beauty. All of our great parks in our large cities and towns are the result of such professional work. Never should such important facilities be entrusted to anyone else. Sometimes in the interest of economy the development of such areas is put in the hands of the municipal park department. Seldom are these people trained designers and, as a result, though use may be achieved beauty is lost. In the long run this is, therefore, false economy.

In designing parks the landscape architect attempts to preserve or create, within the city or nearby, the charm of a natural landscape. Hence in most large parks the design is informal or naturalistic. Certain features, however, like band shells, memorials around which congregations of people may be expected to assemble on occasions, outdoor theaters or amphitheaters, and even large stadia which may be a part of the recreational area of such developments, often need more definite organization than the rural landscape would be likely to provide and hence the areas around these features are customarily designed in a more formal manner even though they may be a part of the over-all informal park design. If they do not become too dominant, such uses and facilities are appropriate park uses.

Most recreational features can, in fact, become an important part of such parks if they are placed in definite areas where they will not interfere or intrude. It should always be remembered that the principal purpose of a large informal park is for pedestrian use so that people can walk about freely, enjoy the scenery undisturbed, read, rest, or meditate among the beauties of nature.

In all his work Frederick Law Olmsted, perhaps our greatest landscape architect and the designer of many of our great parks, followed certain fundamental principles. In park work he always emphasized the contrast between objects seen in the city and objects viewed in the open country. He thought that trimmed trees, flowers in pots, clipped grass, and variegated flower or foliage beds savored of the city or at least the suburb; and he preferred for the purpose of refreshing the city population undulating meadows fringed with trees, quiet, far-stretching pastoral scenery, and groves in which the underbrush and the rough surface of the natural forest was preserved. Paths, roads, resting places and restaurants he regarded as necessary facilities to enable people to enjoy the essential restfulness of park scenery, but he never allowed these artificial features to become the objects of any landscape undertaking, but only its necessary accessories. These principles still hold true today.

Though the principal purpose of park design may be for the pedestrian, drives through the park are permissible when it is large enough so that they do not dominate the scenery. These and a system of paths and trails, not necessarily paralleling them, will often become the framework on which the park design is based.

Ordinarily any piece of property of this extent will need some modification by proper grading to accommodate the various uses to which the various areas will be put, but if the property has any natural features such as good trees or other natural growth, as much of this as possible should be preserved. It is common, today, to say that it is much cheaper to bulldoze an entire area first and then replace the necessary planting. This may, indeed, be cheaper but the end result will not be the same for many, many years. Are we, after all, chiefly concerned with trying to do something on the cheap side? Aren't we, rather, trying to create an area that will remain beautiful as well as useful, something that will add to the attractive appearance of the community and be satisfying to citizens of all ages? As Robert Moses has said, "You can expect cooperation from the public only if you give them the best, that is if you give them something which is obviously suitable, adequate, durable and, perhaps, a little imposing."

In judging a proposed park design that may be offered for citizen approval the following brief discussion of park design may be found helpful. Pleasant views out of the park should be developed and framed by suitable planting, but views into it from the outside should not be encouraged. The whole area may be treated as one scenic unit, but more preferably, it should be divided by groves of trees and appropriate shrub plantings into a series of subareas, each with its particular charm, to be discovered pleasantly as one traverses the park.

The judicious use of water features is desirable and sculpture of the right sort, properly placed, adds interest. Plenty of places to sit down are mandatory and the less conspicuous they are the better, and the more moveable, so that people can get together in social groups or move as occasion requires to enjoy shade or sun or to get out of the wind. Lighting is important but the light standards can just as well be an added attraction as an ugly intrusion. If they remain inconspicuous, buildings for temporary shelter are desirable, but the intrusion into the park of any sort of building, be it a museum, memorial, municipal garage, or whatever, whose function is not primarily a park function should be prevented.

Suitable gateways to give importance to the park entrances are needed and they offer an opportunity for the designer to create something of outstanding beauty. An enclosure of some sort, fence or wall, is probably necessary but it need not be monumental or expensively designed since it will probably be largely hidden by shrub and tree plantings inside the park. If the area is large, service roads through it for commercial and other vehicles may be necessary, but these should be so laid out and designed that they are as nearly invisible from within the park as possible. All these problems and many others involving drainage, water supply, planting design, and maintenance face the park designer who often finds himself confronted by many obstacles, not the least of which is public ignorance and indifference as to what he is trying to accomplish. If he has the intelligent support of a large portion of the citizens of the community his work will be a lot easier and the result a lot better for all concerned.

Outlying Reservations

Wherever and whenever possible communities should acquire undeveloped acreages on their outskirts to be held as reservations with the intention of future more intensive development as parks and recreation areas. These should be tracts of land capable of being developed for use without destroying their primarily rustic or natural appearance. As will be noted elsewhere every municipality has the power and the right to purchase property, even by condemnation if necessary, for the general welfare and use of its people. Not enough of this, at present, is being done and we are fast losing to the builders valuable open spaces which, if preserved, would add immensely to both the enjoyment and appearance of our communities.

The proper development of such reservations is quite different from that appropriate to the areas just discussed. Limited, immediate use may be provided by the creation of adequate parking areas at some convenient point of access to the property but not deep within it, and a system of footpaths or trails. We should be primarily concerned with the preservation of the natural beauties of the property. A step toward the solution of this problem is to exclude from these areas all those uses that require formally graded playing fields or buildings of any considerable size. Roads, paths, and trails can be built of inconspicuous materials leading to areas set aside for picnicking or, if the area is large enough, camping. Nature trails can be set up which are a boon to both Boy and Girl Scouts. It is most important that none of these activities be so concentrated as to be unduly noticeable; they should be arranged to avoid what park people refer to as human erosion, and so as not to destroy or seriously damage the native flora, nor drive away the native fauna.

One of the most serious problems connected with reservations of this type, especially in suburban areas near very large cities, is the influx of city people who crowd out the local inhabitants. When such a situation looms it is imperative to find some means of closing the area to outsiders, an unfriendly thing, perhaps, but a very necessary one. The simplest method of achieving this is through the issuance of passes and limiting the parking space only to those local cars which display a sticker, obtained without cost or for a very small fee, from the proper authorities. Still another is to give very strong support to programs either by the neighboring city, county, state, or even the federal government, to set aside more property and to create expanded facilities to care for large groups of people from the urban areas. After all they should not be denied an opportunity to enjoy the country and every piece of property so set aside and properly developed secures for all of us that much more valuable open space.

8. Conservation for Open Spaces

The preservation of open spaces for their own sake is one of the most widely discussed community problems today. During the past thirty years or so a tremendous and far-reaching change has taken place in the way our towns and cities grow. With the rapid increase in population and the migration of rural people to the urban areas, the city dwellers have fled to the suburbs and beyond in search of more satisfactory conditions in which to live and raise their families. Depending where you are, this movement is variously known as progress, suburban sprawl, invasion of the rabble, flight from blight, and similar descriptive terms. Whatever it may be called it has had and is continuing to have a profound effect on the lives of all of us.

Nothing that has happened to the countryside in the past can compare with the way this movement eats up land. It has progressed now to a point where one can easily imagine an urban-suburban complex coming into existence reaching all the way from Portland, Maine, to Norfolk, Virginia, and inland for some fifty miles or so; another reaching from north of Milwaukee, Wisconsin, to south of Chicago, Illinois; another from San Francisco to San Diego, California, and other, smaller complexes throughout the nation. Farmland, woodland, salt marsh, and open heath are rapidly turning into one housing development after another without separation or breathing space between, all slightly dissimilar but nearly enough alike to produce the most deadening, monotonous urban complex ever seen.

In the name of free enterprise developers have been allowed to gobble up vast amounts of land for housing, dispersed industry, and new shopping facilities to serve the newly spread-out populations. Highway engineers with their elaborate expressways and land-eating clover-leaf intersections and wide rights of way have taken additional acres. Straightening and widening existing highways has taken still more. Arable farmland for market-garden crops near urban centers, a thing we need but which exists only in quite limited quantities, is disappearing so rapidly that conservationists and agricultural economists are quite understandably alarmed lest not enough crop-raising land will be left to support our population at its present standard of living. All this has happened through inadequate planning and almost no controls.

The problem is serious not only from the point of view of economics alone. It is having serious social consequences. People who have moved from the crowded city into what they thought of as the country, to give their families room to live and breathe, soon find themselves in the midst of a built-up suburban neighborhood which, though not perhaps as crowded as the city from which they came, is, nonetheless, becoming more densely populated, more crowded and confused, more remote from quiet countryside and recreational areas than they like. Thus the desirable qualities of suburban living are lost to them and the move from the city turns out to have been a futile one. They have given up the city's advantages, which are many, in exchange for suburban and country values which have been taken away from them, leaving them, to all intents and purposes, in a no-man's-land.

Responsibility for this undesirable situation is usually laid at the door of the speculative builder. He is accused of desecrating the countryside, crowding the land with too many houses, ruining our small country villages into which he moves, cutting down trees, filling up swamps and streams, and in every way doing as much damage as possible for the sake of making a "quick buck." This is only partly true. The speculative builder has indeed committed many crimes but he has remained, by and large, within the law. Hence it behooves us to look at the laws, or lack of them, that govern his activities.

If the local community has not instituted a sound planning program, implemented by modern zoning regulations and subdivision controls, it has only itself to blame when a builder comes and provides housing or commercial buildings, for which he sees a demand, in such a way as to produce for him the most profit. That has always been the American way—unrestrained free enterprise and the devil take the hindmost. This was the way the country was developed and it is only in recent years that people have awakened to what has gone on, and see what is still going on—the tragic waste of the land and its resources in the name of progress. The conservation movement, beginning under Theodore Roosevelt and his friend Gifford Pinchot early in this century and continued under Franklin Roosevelt, has gained momentum and respectability. Much has been accomplished, but much more still remains to be done.

Nor are the people who move from the city to the suburbs entirely blameless for the situation that has developed in the outskirts of most of our cities and towns. They come from areas where many services are provided by the municipal government, "free." Of course these things are paid for in taxes, but people who rent are seldom aware of how much of what they pay goes into municipal services. Nor have they had much direct contact with municipal government. When they arrive in a new suburb they find that some services they are used to are lacking. They also find swamps, marshes, ponds, and streams somewhat terrifying. So they begin demanding that their streets be paved and curbed, sidewalks installed, that garbage collection, police and fire protection be provided and, what interests most here, that swamps be filled or fenced, that streams be confined into drainage ditches or put in pipes underground, that the countryside be put in order and made "safe." Thus they proceed to destroy the very values they came to the country to seek. This may be a passive attitude as well as an active one. Merely to raise no protest when some beautiful natural landscape is destroyed is a shirking of their duty.

Responsibility to plan for future development of our communities, and to educate our people to realize what must be done, rests on every forward-looking municipal administration, every planning board, every garden club, or any other individual or organization that realizes the necessity of preserving the beauty of the countryside for our own enjoyment and that of future generations.

To make a pleasant community, it has always been realized, it is necessary to create a balanced arrangement of built-up and open spaces within the community area. Not always has this principle been consciously acted upon but in going back through history one finds that almost every human community consisted of this combination of buildings and open squares, parks, and gardens.

Under the guidance of Frederick Law Olmsted Boston acquired its magnificent park system, and through him New York City obtained Central and Prospect Parks. Cleveland, Philadelphia, and many other cities did likewise. Olmsted and others with a similar understanding had the ability to enlist the support both of the average citizen and the municipal authorities, without whose cooperation these achievements would have been impossible. The 19th century was a great era of park acquisition and development.

Even though the country had been given a strong impetus

by the Chicago World's Fair of 1893 (designed by Olmsted and Daniel H. Burnham), the enthusiasm for acquiring and developing parks in our communities suffered a decline. Not enough additional land was set aside to keep up with the rapidly growing population with the result that most communities find themselves today far behind in providing parks and other open spaces needed by their populations. The demand for more and more housing and accessory commercial and industrial developments that go with it has pushed aside considerations for maintaining a proper balance between built-up and open spaces.

Realizing this need, state legislatures have enacted laws that permit local municipal governments to delegate to their planning boards the power not only to pass on and approve or disapprove land subdivision maps, but to require, while doing so, that a reasonable proportion of the land be set aside as a public park. This legislation, however, has not accomplished much. In the first place the power to require the donation of park land by the developer was made permissive rather than mandatory and, since many communities, particularly the small ones, were loath to undertake the development and maintenance of these small parks, it was invoked only occasionally and rather timidly.

Some planning boards tried hard to put this program into effect but they were handicapped by resistance from the developers who hated to give up valuable land, the opposition of elected officials who feared that the cost of equipping and maintaining these areas would raise taxes and make them, the officials, unpopular, and the apathy of the general public which took little or no interest in the matter. A further weakness in the program was that the park lands could be acquired only when and where a new development was proposed. More often than not this was a location where, from the point of view of the community as a whole, no park was needed. It made no provision for a communitywide park program by which areas suitable in size, in suitable locations, could be acquired.

Because in many communities growth and development have progressed to a point where little or no open space remains within the corporate boundaries of the municipality, it is necessary that the community seek to obtain or control land outside its legal boundaries. This may prove to be difficult. Neighboring communities may resent an invasion of their precincts, especially if the land being sequestered is to be removed from the tax rolls. Officials of these neighboring municipalities may resist forceably, or at least refuse their cooperation.

To help combat this situation some states have instituted joint or cooperative planning legislation to make it possible for neighboring communities to join together in a comprehensive program of land acquisition and development. County agencies may also be formed to help out the local situation plagued by the arbitrary boundaries of towns, villages, or special districts. A recent development of great importance is legislation in a number of the northeastern states empowering communities to acquire open-space areas for preservation without having to commit themselves to outright purchase or immediate development.

Since many communities cannot afford the outright purchase price of these desirable areas, these new powers and provisions of the law should be most valuable. Under these powers the communities can save areas of beautiful scenery, obtain access to beach and waterfront properties to be developed later for recreational purposes if the need arises, and to provide necessary breathing spaces between closely built-up areas. All this can be done well within the means of the community.

In many communities areas exist that have been jumped over or otherwise neglected in the march of development, or that were put to uses now obsolete. One thinks of the old wharf areas along our rivers and harbors now no longer intensively used; derelict railroad shop and yard areas, or abandoned railroad rights of way; steep, rocky ravines and stream beds, or even stretches of marshland. These areas are not usually very expensive to acquire as they are too difficult to develop for profitable purposes. But they can be cleaned up and left as open spaces to the great beautification of the community.

It is highly desirable, of course, that all remaining open areas within a community be acquired and preserved as open space, either useful or not, but it is equally important to obtain possession or control of desirable areas outside the community's boundaries. These need not be contiguous with it, nor even nearby, although this is desirable. They should, however, be properties or areas that have some outstanding characteristic. They may be a particularly picturesque mountain or crag; a fine waterfall with its accompanying gorge or ravine; a unique seaside area with sand dunes or long, open stretches of beach; an untouched stretch of farmland and hills; or a quiet pond surrounded by woodland; or a forested area which has not been cut over. The point is that they should be sufficiently eye-arresting to make people want to go to see and enjoy them. Whatever they are, they should be preserved and left alone in their natural beauty.

Efforts to "develop" such areas for whatever purpose tend to destroy those qualities that made them desirable subjects for preservation in the first place. Access to them must be provided and a place where cars can be parked sometimes increases their worth. This does not mean that a system of roads or even paths through the area is necessary, nor need universal provision of picnic areas, camp sites and the like be made, although there are opportunities for this sort of development without destroying the original charm.

Any one of several related powers may be used by the municipality or regional agency to acquire open space. The authorities may, of course, acquire such sites by outright purchase. If the voters in a single municipality or region approve by referendum a project to purchase land, and appropriate the money, the acquisition is simple.

If the owner refuses to sell, the municipality may invoke the power of eminent domain under which the property would be acquired by condemnation. To be valid such procedures must be able to justify the acquisition as in the public interest but this should not prove to be difficult because a wide variety of purposes have been recognized by the courts as a matter of public benefit. When property is taken in this manner, the owner is offered a fair price based on the findings of qualified appraisers. If he accepts this, the process of acquisition may proceed. If he refuses, a condemnation commission will be established which will arbitrate the matter and establish a price which the owner is bound to accept unless he wants to continue the fight in the courts. He has a right to do this, but the outcome is uncertain and the cost considerable. No one may be deprived of his property, however, without due process of law. These procedures are both well established—outright purchase and acquisition by eminent domain.

What is new, however, are (1) the right to buy and lease back with limited-use provisions; (2) the power to buy rights of use or easement, in which case the title to the property remains with the original owner; (3) tax-abatement plans to ease the burden of loss, or certain rights to the owner; and (4) the freezing of assessments to prevent a rise in taxes in lieu of payment for concessions.

Broad legislation embodying these new powers has been enacted in Connecticut, New York, New Jersey, and Pennsylvania. The Connecticut law is probably the most comprehensive. Enacted in 1962, it provides money for state acquisition and development projects and also for a town incentive program under which local governments may receive grants-in-aid for open-space acquisition or control of various properties including wetlands, historic district preservation, conservation easements for stream valley protection, as well as for the usual recreational purposes.

The New Jersey, New York, and Pennsylvania programs are oriented toward conservation of open space on a statewide basis rather than a local one but, of course, local communities near which land is acquired would benefit from them. In Massachusetts an arrangement has been made whereby taxes on commercially operated forest land do not fall due until the timber crop is harvested. This encourages the owners to delay cutting until the trees reach their maturity, instead of cutting immature trees to obtain current income.

Under the first of these powers enumerated above, the land would have to be acquired by the time-honored procedures of outright purchase or eminent domain. Let us take a hypothetical case. Suppose that near a community a beautiful valley devoted to dairy farming exists. It lies directly in the path of development and unless something is done it will soon be subdivided and developed for housing or industry. It is a place people see and enjoy from some vantage point along an important highway. It is an area that some time in the future might be advantageously developed for community recreational purposes but it is not presently needed for that purpose. The community may acquire it and then lease it back to the former owner, or to someone else, to be operated exclusively as a dairy farm with no changes in use, demolition of old or erection of new buildings, removal of trees or forest, installation of billboards, or highway fringe business establishments being permitted. The only cost is the loss of tax revenue on the land and interest on the investment less, of course, the rental which would probably be nominal. Not a great amount in view of the benefits derived. When, and if, the community ever needs the land for any purpose, the lease can be terminated and the public comes into full possession.

Under the second type of procedure in which the title to the property does not change hands, but the community acquires certain specific rights over it, an agreement is drawn up between the community and the owner under which he gives up the right to sell, develop, or radically change the character of or the use of the property. On its part the community agrees to pay either a lump sum or an annual rental. Such agreements should be made for a definite term of years rather than in perpetuity to allow for revision on the agreement if conditions governing it should change.

The third method is often used as a part of a comprehensive planning program. It is really a variant of the second method outlined above. Instead of a lump sum or annual rental in payment by the community to the owner, an agreement is entered into under which the community agrees to reduce the taxes on the property as compensation for restricting its free use by the owner.

The fourth method is a still further variant under which, instead of reducing taxes, the community agrees not to raise the assessment on the property no matter what may happen to the value of neighboring land, thus freezing the taxes at about their present level—unless, of course, the rate is increased.

Which method of procedure to use will depend on numerous factors such as the financial condition of the acquiring community, the willingness of the owners to enter into agreements, the urgency of the situation, and so on. Each community will have to decide for itself how to proceed in connection with each separate parcel of land being considered, but any one of these methods will enable a community to avail itself of open space before it is too late.

Another way of acquiring desirable open space is by deed

of gift. Often large areas of unoccupied country owned by persons or corporations who have no use for them may be obtained in this manner. The areas may have been inherited or acquired for their mineral resources which have been extracted, or their forests which have been cut. Continuing to pay taxes on such land is often a losing proposition and, if properly approached, the owners of many such lands could be induced to deed the property to either the state or the local municipality. Many such areas have great scenic value and quite a few are located within practical distance of communities that could take good advantage of them.

Sometimes groups of interested citizens will form an association for the purpose of obtaining title to desirable properties that otherwise might fall into the hands of commercial interests. Such an organization is the Nature Conservancy whose membership is nationwide and which has been able in a number of ways to assist local groups interested in obtaining control of valuable scenic and natural resource areas that should be conserved. It will, under certain circumstances, accept custody of land. Such land must have recognized value as a natural area and be so located that it can be maintained. It provides for a continuity of policy regarding the care of such lands, helps finance permanent preservation through the income from its endowment fund and other fund-raising efforts. It helps defend such areas from those who would exploit them for personal benefits.

Another organization is California's famous Sierra Club founded in 1892 by John Muir, the noted naturalist, primarily to protect the Yosemite National Park from encroaching ranchers. The Sierra Club has grown to a membership of over 24,000 divided among 17 chapters scattered over the far West, the Great Lakes region and the Atlantic coast. It is said to be the most powerful citizens' conservation organization in the country. Any community struggling to preserve some valuable scenic area or one rich in irreplaceable natural resources would be well advised to enlist its interest and assistance.

As this is being written, we are confronted by the proposal to run a freeway through the National Tribute Grove which was established in Jedediah Smith State Park in California to honor many of those who fought in both World Wars. This outrageous proposal that would also destroy many of the relatively few redwood trees remaining unmolested by the lumber interests should be emphatically defeated, and those proposing it should be made clearly aware that though the country wants and needs highways, it does not need them at the expense of everything else. The automobile should remain a contributor to the good life, not the agent of its destruction, and those who serve it must realize that their proposals cannot be permitted always to take precedence over all other considerations.

Of course any attempt to acquire open land will be opposed by someone. If it is land that lies in the path of the normal development of some suburban or rural community, the owner is likely to feel that he will get more for his land if he holds it for awhile and sells to a developer than he will if he sells to the municipality. Real estate and commercial interests will also oppose the proposition for obvious reasons. If it is a state or federal proposal, lobbies at the state capitol or in Washington will get to work to prevent its adoption. Citizens' groups interested in furthering such proposals must realize that to offset these opposing forces they must also organize, propagandize, educate, and lobby for all they are worth. It may cost them a great deal of time and some money but it is the only way things can be accomplished in our civilization today. Programs for land acquisition, whether they originate in the municipal administration, the planning board, or in a citizens' group should, if they are sound, be vigorously and consistently supported by everyone interested in civic beautification and development. Only through strong citizen support can the program succeed.

Open space may be acquired not only as such and by individual communities but also incidentally in connection with projects involving higher authority and extending over a wide area. One such is the Federal Interstate Highway System now under construction. These highways may in many places acquire very wide rights of way, especially through nonbuilt-up areas thus permitting wider median strips, separation of roadways, and ample side slopes. Thus open space is obtained and made a permanent feature of the landscape. Great care should also be exercised in laying out new highways so that they do not damage nearby, existing communities or cut established neighborhoods in two. The social consequences of poorly located highways have not been fully appreciated nor have communities being affected taken sufficiently firm stands to prevent serious damage. The fact that these highways open up to view large areas that were formerly invisible from any highway should be taken into consideration and provision made for enjoying what has been revealed. Overlooks along these new highways should be provided at more frequent intervals for this purpose.

The tendency to use existing publicly owned lands, such as parks and forest reservations, for highway purposes is something that must be constantly kept in mind by those concerned with civic beauty. This type of encroachment should always be resisted and, if possible, prevented. In a recent brochure outlining the policies of the American Society of Landscape Architects it is stated that policy number one of the society is opposition "to the construction of freeways or other nonpark road facilities and the erection of buildings or other structures in public parks, shoreline reservations or civic plazas excepting only those roads and structures necessary for the administration of or the public's increased enjoyment or recreational use of such areas."

Open land in urban areas is indispensable to community existence as a matter of public health and welfare. Nevertheless state and city governments often abet this evil practice of encroaching on park land because it saves tax dollars. If we are to have a pleasant environment for living we must stop thinking in terms of doing everything the cheapest way. We must do it the best way for all concerned. This does not mean extravagance, which is certainly not the best way for all concerned, nor does it mean the cheapest way which, in the long run, tends to become the most expensive way. Sound planning will assure that whatever is done is done well, properly located, and economically built. Under the police power the government of the community not only has a duty to promote those things that will enhance the "health, safety and general welfare" of the community, but to avoid and oppose those things which will endanger them. Over the years the courts have broadened the powers of the community under the police power so that almost anything that can be demonstrated to be in the community's general welfare can be undertaken or required of the municipal government. This is something all those interested in civic beautification and development should remember.

Other open-space areas, usually acquired by the state or federal government, but the existence of which may be of great benefit to a local community, are such things as wildlife sanctuaries, water-supply protection areas, flood-control areas, and other large scale engineering projects of that type, wetlands, marginal lands too poor for profitable agricultural use, flood-plain areas unsafe for residential use, lakes, ponds, and river valleys. State and federal park projects covering mountain, forest, and shoreline areas on a large scale, developed either as recreational facilities or held as wilderness reservations, are preserving valuable areas, but many more of such sites should be acquired. For some reason the federal programs of land acquisition for these purposes has slowed down during recent years. Pressure should be brought to bear on the federal government for a reactivation of this conservation program.

The establishment of state forests and parks is another avenue of approach to the open-space program. These facilities are usually either operated by the state as controlled commercial forests, or as camping and recreational parks. New York and other northeastern states, as well as several western ones, have large state forest areas, well managed so that they are profitable but also preserved from desecration and destruction. Many states have fine state park programs but as population increases, all of these need to be extended or their number increased so as to avoid overcrowding and human erosion.

Difference of opinion will always arise over how to deal with a particular open area once it is acquired. The first principle is, of course, to preserve intact the natural character of the property. Once land is acquired by a municipality, or by an individual for that matter, an urge to clean up and put it to use immediately arises. In the case of land acquired for the purpose of preserving scenic beauty or providing open space merely as such, this impulse should be resisted. More harm can be done by ill-advised clean-up and improvement programs than can be imagined. Obviously accumulations of junk, existing billboards, tumble-down buildings and the like, should be removed and, if the area is forested, dead and fallen trees or accumulations of slash resulting from lumbering operations, which might constitute a fire hazard, should be taken care of. On such properties, however, little else need be done. It is generally unwise to develop roads and paths through these areas, to provide picnic tables or camp sites, but adequate space should be provided from which people can take advantage of spectacular views. These might be spacious overlook parking areas. Sometimes a neat sign telling something about the site, its history, unique topographical or geological features, or how it was obtained for public use, might be provided.

If the community lacks adequate park areas and facilities within its boundaries, and many of them do, land acquired outside it may properly be more intensively developed for use as a recreation area of one sort or another but at the same time keeping as much of its natural character as possible. Golf courses, ski areas, and similar large scale activities can sometimes be accommodated but more intensive recreational facilities like athletic fields, swimming pools, or camp areas should be undertaken only with the greatest care. If properly located these things need not destroy the primary value of the property. This is largely a matter of design and the development of such areas should never be left to chance but be placed in the hands of competent persons with an appreciation and love of the natural landscape which they will be certain to protect. Usually the development of such an area for recreation should be undertaken gradually rather than all at once to permit nature to repair the unavoidable scars such a development will make.

When areas are acquired primarily as conservation projects the approach will have to be somewhat different. Nothing should be permitted that will interfere with the preservation and protection of whatever it may be that is being conserved. If it is wildlife, then no hunting can be permitted and very little access by humans or domestic animals. Provision for occasional feeding may be necessary, or even some shelter. The management of bird sanctuaries requires that these areas remain undisturbed, that the kind of growth suitable for nesting sites be encouraged as well as that which produces a source of food supply. The Audubon Society, an organization devoted to the preservation of bird life, has developed a program of management for such areas and is happy to cooperate with local authorities in establishing and maintaining bird sanctuaries for conservation and study. In the great flyways vast numbers of migratory birds pass back and forth from their nesting grounds in the North to their winter quarters in the South. Large areas have already been set aside as resting places for them during migrations but much more needs to be done if these valuable birds are to live and multiply.

If it is flora that is to be protected, conditions that would adversely affect the growth of desirable plants cannot be permitted to exist. For example the raising of the water table to create a lake might also create conditions incompatible with the growth requirements of many plants. Nor should the growth in a natural woodland be permitted to become so dense as to shade out many desirable species of plants.

Water conservation requires special programs of reforestation and forest preservation to prevent too rapid run-off, and the construction of flood-control or water-storage dams may be advisable but these should be constructed in such a location and manner that they do not destroy the natural landscape any more than can be helped. In many parts of the South small lakes have been created by damming up small stream valleys. These lakes are not only ornamental but, when stocked with fish, become an important economic asset. In other parts of the country fishing streams have been stocked with trout and other fish, but if they are to continue to supply sportsmen with good fishing they must be protected from water pollution from any source and unnecessary disturbance by highway construction. In some states small access areas to fishing streams have been provided where fishermen can park their cars while enjoying this sport, thus leaving the highways uncluttered. These access areas can add to civic beauty if well cared for, but if they are not they soon become eyesores.

Some states, particularly Virginia, have taken over vast acreages of so-called marginal land that has been damaged by careless agricultural practices of the past. This land is valuable for reforestation and by taking it over the state can enter into such projects, prevent ill-advised scattered attempts at subsistence farming projects, which are bound to fail, and at the same time preserve valuable open space for future generations. Fire control in such reforested areas is of great importance and is often aided by the opening up of adequate fire lanes through the forested land, or plowing strips along the roadsides or along open fields. Generally such areas are closed to the public during prolonged dry periods when the hazard of fire is great.

Because so much of this important natural resource has been, and is still being, destroyed one of the great needs in many areas is a reforestation program. On almost any land held for scenic or open space purposes, a carefully designed reforestation program can and should be instituted and consistently pursued. Even rather small areas need to have proper forestry practices applied to them. Old trees will always be dying or being blown down and these need to be replaced. This applies equally to urban park situations. In forest reservations or larger scenic areas the reforestation of barren, open lands, or replacement of trees where lumbering has been permitted, should never be neglected. Some of the lumber and pulp companies have undertaken vast projects of this sort on their own initiative, and the states and federal government carry on programs on land they control.

To sum up this important subject of the acquisition and preservation of open land we quote from the Foreword of Stewart L. Udall's important book *The Quiet Crisis*: "America today stands poised on a pinnacle of wealth and power, yet we live in a land of vanishing beauty, of increasing ugliness, of shrinking open space, and of an over-all environment that is diminishing daily by pollution and noise and blight." He further states that it is not too late to repair some of the mistakes of the past and "to make America a green and pleasant—and productive—land."

9. Street Trees and Community Planting

The towns and villages of America have always been known for their multitude of beautiful trees. It has been said that a home without trees is charmless; a street without trees is shadeless; a park without trees is purposeless; and a country without trees is hopeless. Nevertheless we are beginning to fear that, with the possible exception of garden-club members, very few people appreciate trees. Certainly most municipal officials have little regard for them when they are in the way of a street widening or the clearing of a piece of land, or if their roots tend to raise the pavement or clog up drains. Highway engineers abhor them, claiming that they litter the highway with branches, twigs, and leaves and, in the colder sections, create hazardous icing conditions on the roadway. Utility companies have little regard for them because they interfere with their overhead wires and sometimes their underground pipes and conduits. They are, nevertheless, more important than any of these considerations and should receive due and proper attention.

There was a time in the development of this country when all streets and most highways were tree lined, and we can recall many pleasant stretches that tunneled under magnificent double avenues of oak, maple, and elm trees. The old

113

idea was to replace, to some extent, forests that had originally covered the area. Trees were often, therefore, planted much too close to the roadway and to each other. Our purpose today is to beautify the area through careful selection of trees to fit existing conditions. It must be admitted, however, that still too many new streets and highways are left treeless and barren, windy and bereft of areas of shade and shadow to temper the glare of the midday sun.

Even in those towns and villages where trees exist along the streets and highways, old age, storms, diseases, and insect pests as well as ill-advised pruning have often ruined their appearance so that many have to be removed. Such trees should be promptly replaced with young and vigorous stock selected for beauty and suitability to the local conditions. Existing conditions of space, soil, climate, and the presence of overhead wires or underground utilities, must be kept in mind so that the trees may grow naturally to maturity.

Every community should have an official street-tree program implemented by a street-tree ordinance properly drawn and properly enforced, preferably by a competent arborist acting as tree warden. In the absence of such an ordinance some interested group, such as a garden club or other organization interested in civic beautification, should form a tree committee to bring pressure to bear in the right quarters to the end that the existing trees be properly maintained or removed and replaced when necessary, and to work toward the eventual adoption of a proper tree ordinance.

Much of the work of such a tree committee should be educational starting, perhaps, in the schools to develop a better understanding of the importance of trees in civic beautification. In 1872 the state of Nebraska observed the first Arbor Day and as a result over a million trees were planted. Since then this day has been observed in many states and is, in fact, a legal holiday in some. But aside from creating one more holiday not enough is being done to impress the public, especially the children of school age, with the importance of continued tree planting.

One of the first things that a tree committee should do is to make a survey of the existing trees in the town. This is the true foundation of a good street-tree program. In this survey those trees that are in good condition and are to remain should be noted as well as those that should be removed or given some attention and, of course, areas where new trees are needed should be stressed. With such information a street-tree map of the whole community can be made and documented according to the various site factors including width of streets, the setback of buildings, the width of the planting strips (variously called tree lawns and neutral strips, the areas between the sidewalk or property line and the roadway), locations of utilities (overhead wires and street lights), and many others that will control the types and size of the trees best suited for a particular location.

Trees can be listed according to size at maturity (their height and spread); their form (round-headed, oval, vase-shaped, pyramidal, or fastigiate); their hardiness (suitability to existing soil and climatic conditions); their rate of growth; their outstanding characteristics (root system, foliage, flowers, and fruit); and their resistance to insect and disease attacks and urban conditions (drought and air pollution). These considerations will determine the choice of varieties. Because young trees are small and may appear insignificant a temptation to plant them too close together exists. In determining spacing the size of the tree at maturity should be the governing criterion.

In recent years the various utility companies have stressed the planting of smaller-growing trees, the so-called secondaries, generally of a floriferous nature. Granted that the use of such trees does create a very beautiful display of color at certain seasons and that they greatly reduce the amount of tree pruning that the utility companies may have to do in later years, they are not as suitable for street-tree use as those whose habit of growth is such that they will fill the space available within a reasonable time and produce a pleasing prospect in harmony with adjacent properties and other growing plants.

These secondaries like the flowering dogwood, cercis, flowering crabs, or other flowering fruits, are much better suited to roadside planting either as specimens or in groups or among other plants placed some distance from the roadway where they may be seen and admired. These can also be used to advantage when planted in the mall between roadways, or along pedestrian and shopping malls where space is at a premium.

The American Society of Landscape Architects (ASLA) has disapproved, as a policy, the use of miniature species or horticultural forms except where special design considerations dictate their use. Neither do they approve of the use of short-lived trees, untried species of unknown endurance, trees requiring frequent spraying, nor the use of small trees merely as a means of reducing pruning costs when larger types would be more attractive. Naturally this society also recommends that a tree-planting plan with its accompanying regulations be drawn by properly trained persons. A tree committee might, therefore, be well advised to secure professional help in the preparation of their tree-planting plan thereby creating greater interest and the possibility of obtaining more adequate financial backing.

On very wide streets, boulevards, and those with a center mall between traffic lanes, the larger and often more beautiful shade trees, like the various maples, oaks, lindens, and elms, should be used. These usually look best when planted opposite each other to create a double avenue effect. If the street is very wide and has a median parked area three, or even four, rows of trees can be planted although this is rarely possible or desirable. It goes back to the old idea of attempted reforestation on the area instead of a designed landscape treatment. On narrower, yet fairly wide streets, the shade trees can be planted alternately rather than opposite each other, thus gaining more room for future growth. The setbacks of buildings has a direct influence on the placement of street trees and where buildings are set fifty to a hundred feet or more from the building lines and have wide open lawns it is wiser to plant shade trees on private property, with permission of course, rather than between the property line and the roadway. When so placed the tree has a better chance to grow for it can obtain more food and moisture and, as it develops, it will not interfere with the utility wires. Even when trees are planted on private property and so near the property line that they can serve as street trees, the street-tree ordinance should be so worded as to place such trees under the jurisdiction of the tree warden.

On narrow streets shade trees will have to be of the narrow-growing oval-headed, pyramidal, or fastigiate types whose branches, even at maturity, will not be too widespread, like the ginkgo, columnar sugar and red maples, the erect Norway maple (*Acer platanoides erectum*), or the pyramidal European hornbeam. This type of tree is not only well suited to narrow residential streets but of especial value in the built-up business areas.

It should be emphasized that more can be done to improve commercial and industrial areas by the judicious use of trees in such places than in any other way. These areas tend to be bleak and, especially in hot weather, they can be intensely uncomfortable. Well-placed trees shading the pedestrian ways are most welcome. They cannot be used successfully, however, unless adequate space is provided both for their roots and the natural spread of their branches. If they are going to rub against buildings or obliterate signs by their foliage the businessmen are not going to like them and will work diligently for their removal. The choice of the right tree may overcome some of these objections. In European cities it is customary to keep such trees severely clipped both for practical reasons and for aesthetic ones as well. Europeans seem to admire clipped allées of plane trees, horse chestnuts, and maples, whereas Americans seem to react violently against any such restraint of natural tree growth. It seems to these writers that the European system has, so far, produced more pleasing results in these closely confined areas we are discussing than the American habit of permitting unrestrained growth.

The problems of street trees and advertising signs in business areas are inextricably intermixed. Every businessman seems to feel that he should not only erect on his establishment the largest possible sign done up in the most brilliant colors, but also that this sign must be visible from the greatest possible distance. When, however, the community decides that it wants its business section to be attractive, green, and shady and decides to plant street trees along its business streets, a conflict is immediately produced. Many battles have been fought over this issue with victory occasionally to the businessman and occasionally to those who have the beautification of their community as their objective. Usually it ends in a draw with a few trees permitted and only the most offensive signs removed.

If advertising signs are confined to the face of buildings, there is no reason why a proper street-tree planting program cannot be adopted, even in the business district, to everyone's advantage. Once the businessman finds his customers thronging the street even on hot, sunny days because they are grateful for the shade, he will realize that flourishing street trees bring in more business than garish signs.

Whether to use a single variety of tree to a street or to mix them is largely a matter of taste. Either system works well. A change from one species to another often adds variety and interest. Years ago it was a common practice to interplant the desirable species with less desirable but quick-growing ones so as to produce more immediate effect. The danger in this sort of planting is that unless the quick-growing, short-lived species are removed in time, the more desirable and permanent trees lack a proper amount of space for development. People become rather sentimental over trees, even the less desirable ones, and an uproar usually results when their necessary removal is even suggested. Such quick-growing trees, like the poplars and soft maples, are weak-wooded and liable to storm damage. They are also often the prey of insects or diseases which, in time, mar their appearance.

Many common ornamental or forest trees should never be used for street-tree purposes. This group includes all those that are not only weak-wooded and short-lived but also those that do not develop strong, deep root systems and are frequently uprooted or seriously damaged by storms, or that create an unusually serious litter problem for the highway department. Trees that produce abundant blossoms and fruits, dropping this litter on the streets and sidewalks, should be avoided because they are a nuisance to pedestrians.

Street trees should be hardy and able to survive the very difficult conditions found in urban, and even some suburban, streets. America is a very large country with a wide variety of climatic and soil conditions and not all trees, desirable though they may be in one location, will serve equally well in all locations. In making a selection, therefore, advice should be asked from local authorities such as nurseries, state schools of agriculture, or County Agents of such institutions.

The cost of a tree-planting program should be borne by the whole community being benefited. When no tree ordinance has been put into effect, the municipal officials often include varying amounts of money in their annual budget for tree planting to be done by the highway department under the supervision of the tree committee. After-planting care becomes an obligation of the municipality. In communities where no funds are made available for tree planting, they can be raised by various means including contributions from individuals or organizations. The planting of street trees, however, does not complete the work of an interested tree committee even though they have also succeeded in getting a proper tree ordinance enacted into law. It is necessary to continue the committee in existence to see that such an ordinance is enforced.

The after-care of street trees is no less important than their planting. This includes both proper feeding and proper pruning. When street trees are left to grow naturally they become, especially in wet weather, hazards to both automobile and pedestrian traffic because of low, overhanging branches. A height of eight feet clearance over sidewalks and thirteen feet over roadways is the standard requirement. Where utility wires are encountered, trees must be either cut back to provide the necessary clearance or opened up so that the wires may pass through, which is a more generally approved method but one that must be undertaken with the greatest of care and restraint. Because some of the firms whose principal activity is the clearing of wires for the utility companies are quite naturally more interested in providing clearance than in the preservation of the appearance of trees, their work should be watched and supervised. Other firms have done, and are doing, admirable work in this field.

Other Types of Public Planting

Street trees are not the only type of planting that creates civic beauty. All other public plantings whether along streets, around public buildings, or used to embellish industrial and commercial establishments, contribute to the total picture of the community. Much of this planting is tastelessly done and poorly maintained.

Examples that prove the contrary to be true come to mind. One thinks of the planting around the Lincoln Memorial and the Supreme Court Building in Washington, both of which are magnificent. The reason these plantings are successful is not because of the particular varieties of plants used, nor particularly because they are healthy and vigorous, though of course they are. The reason for their great beauty is that they are in scale with the buildings they accompany. This is the important point in connection with all planting around or near a large building, be it a public structure or a privately owned factory or anything else. Most such plantings are woefully out of scale. Too many plants, too small in size, too fine in texture, too indefinite in form, have been used. For this sort of work a few plants of the right form, color, and texture will be found to be much more suitable than a large number of small plants of indefinite form, fine texture, and neutral color.

It is very easy to fall into the error of producing this sort of characterless planting. The cost of large plants is considerable and the right ones for a particular position are often hard to find. Small plants can be obtained more easily, and one always hopes they will eventually grow to produce the proper ultimate height. Meanwhile, however, the planting appears to be trivial, out of scale with the building it would adorn, and ineffective. If it ever does grow into what it should, it is the exception rather than the rule. A few large plants, though they are costly, will immediately produce the appropriate atmosphere, the ideal composition one has been working toward. In the long run, surprisingly perhaps, they will not cost any more than the multitude of small ones often planted in their stead.

Not only will large plants be more in scale and so produce

the desired effect, but the temptation to use too many varieties in order to produce interest will have been eliminated. Only a very few varieties of plants should be used to create a composition. One should never attempt to create an arboretum, however tempting such an idea might be. This is one of the great troubles in plantings done, with the best of intentions, by enthusiastic groups who are interested in horticulture. They attempt to use too many species. Plants should be selected for this sort of planting on the basis of suitability, size, form, texture, and the color of their foliage and, above all, how they will relate to and compose with the building near which they are to be used. It should never be the purpose of these plantings to detract from the architectural character of the building by calling undue attention to themselves. Lavish and violent color, too many spiky emphatic forms, too lush a foliage mass, or just too much planting altogether, are not what is needed. The purpose of the planting about a public building, or any building for that matter, is to accent and heighten the effect of the architecture, not to cover it up or compete with it.

As we go about the country it seems to us that public buildings and modern industrial plants which have taken on something of the character of public buildings, are either overplanted, or not planted at all. Many schools today are standing in bare fields without a tree or a bush anywhere to be seen. Many factories that now appear ugly would take on a much more acceptable appearance if they had some appropriate planting. On the other hand, many a school arises from a fringe of evergreen shrubs which have been planted around the entire periphery of the building—a dull, monotonous thing to have done—or a factory is smothered in greenery with the intent, by the owners, to increase public acceptance of it as a community asset rather than a liability as it would formerly have been considered. Both lack of enough planting and the presence of too much of it operate against the achievement of civic beauty.

We are often asked what to plant in front of the new library, city hall, or some other public building. Such questions can only be answered in the most general terms because too many conditions of soil, climate, exposure, maintenance and, above all, personal preferences enter into a choice. It is possible, however, to make a few suggestions which are really principles that can be applied and adapted to specific situations.

Most of the older public buildings of whatever sort, city hall, courthouse, library, fire station and the like, were built in one of the traditional architectural styles. Hence they are likely to have a balanced facade, with the entrance in the middle, and to stand on rather high basements or foundations. Often numerous areaways have been built along the front of such buildings to light basement windows. Rarely are there heavy cornices, though sometimes they do exist and have to be taken into consideration if they project out over the planting area. Windows are usually fairly high up from the ground and evenly spaced. Columns, pilasters, and porticos frequently form the basis of the composition. Such a building needs some planting on either side of the main entrance to call attention to this usually fairly elaborate architectural detail, and perhaps at the corners of the building to soften this architectural line. It rarely needs anything else. It should never have a foundation planting in the manner of a suburban residence. Because of the areaways it may be necessary to use some very low planting along the front to hide their ugliness but this should never be high enough to be noticeable for itself. The areas between the building and walks are usually best planted with one of the ground covers because in such places lawns are hard to maintain. Plants chosen for the principal groups should be of a form compatible with the architectural style of the building—probably one fairly tall, emphatic form and a few rounded ones nearby to carry the lines of the composition down to the ground. This emphatic form would vary from the thinnest, most columnar shapes like some arvorvitae, suitable for a building in the Italian Renaissance style, to a broadly rounded cone shape more suitable for a building in the Greek Doric style, or in the later English Tudor and Elizabethan manner. One cannot be more specific and the examples merely indicate that careful selection is necessary with the style of the building always in mind.

Most buildings in the modern or contemporary style, on the other hand, are unsymmetrical with the main entrance off to one side or at the corner. They may be heavy with wide overhanging eaves, in which case no planting should be located close to the building. They are likely to be set closer to the ground than buildings in the older styles and their windows are lower to the ground and often irregularly spaced. Columns, pilasters and porticos, and other surface ornamentations, are likely to be entirely absent.

Such buildings cannot accept symmetrical, balanced plantings. These would conflict with the architectural composition of the facade. Often large, blank wall surfaces are found that call for a mass planting in front of them to relieve monotony. No foundation planting of any sort is needed or desirable. The common habit of planting an evergreen hedge all across the front of a building only tends to disassociate the building from the ground on which it stands. Vines on the masonry may help to soften its appearance but they should not be allowed to cover too much of it. Very few plants, really, are needed but what few are used should be chosen carefully for their form and color to blend with that of the building, or to contrast with it if that is deemed desirable. Here, too, the plant groups should be so located that they actually embellish but do not hide the outstanding architectural features. Often plant groups, especially trees, can be used to the best advantage away from the building but so positioned that they enframe the structure and help blend it into the surrounding landscape.

Most planting used to embellish a public or a semipublic structure is evergreen. However, deciduous material can be used successfully and in some parts of the country, where evergreen materials do not thrive, this is the only sort of material that can be used successfully. Because most deciduous shrubs and trees grow more rapidly than do evergreen varieties, more care must be taken in their selection and placement so that the planting does not too rapidly outgrow the spaces allotted to it. When, and if, this does happen and plants overhang walkways or hide windows, they should be ruthlessly removed and discarded and new ones of the same or more appropriate sorts put in their place. If this is not done, someone will surely come along and shear them to get them out of the way. This treatment is fatal to any composition that aspires to any artistic quality. You simply cannot make an effective composition out of a few rounded blobs of deciduous shrubbery. Not only that, but the plants themselves, from a point of view of their health and future growth, do not respond happily to this treatment. Removal and replacement is the only proper procedure.

Other public planting than that around buildings is the sort of thing one sees along parked streets, in the center malls of divided highways, in small areas at street intersections and the like. Here proper selection of material and its arrangement into effective compositions is of even greater importance, for such plantings are usually seen from several angles. Form, texture, and the color of foliage is still important and the color of bloom plays a more important role than in plantations near buildings. Many of our southern cities and towns have made a reputation with their azalea plantings. Compact plants like these look well the year around even when they are not in bloom and they are slow-growing enough to warrant their use in fairly large masses. Many other plants, however, are attractive mainly when they are in bloom but have long periods when they are not at all beautiful, for example, the crape myrtle, another plant widely used in the South for street plantings.

In the more northern areas the problem of snow removal makes the choice of material and its placement more difficult, for much of it may have to withstand snow piled on or around it for several weeks. Here the small trees like the dogwood and the various flowering crabs and such shrubs as lilac, forsythia, and spirea will often be found suitable for such a use.

In the smaller areas, such as at the intersection of streets where it is imperative not to block the line of vision of traffic, only low-growing material can be successfully used. In recent years many garden clubs have instituted a planting program for these small areas which calls for bulbs in the spring followed by annuals, especially glowing beds of geraniums or petunias. Any ambitious community can institute a program of beautification through the means of civic planting of this sort. Starting in a small way these plantings can be gradually expanded year by year until the whole town becomes known for its flower-decked streets and highways. Once such a program gains impetus, the municipality itself can often be induced to take part through its highway or park department.

10. Roadside Rehabilitation and Beautification

Because people have begun to realize that the condition of the roadsides throughout the country has become deplorable, organizations have been formed to try to do something about it. The Keep America Beautiful organization and the Roadside Development committees, active in many states and sponsored by the National Council of State Garden Clubs, are doing a great deal, not only to improve existing conditions but to make the public aware of the need and to play a part in the work. Pennsylvania, for example, has one of the most outstanding and active Roadside committees which is not only aware of the importance of roadside improvement but is doing a tremendous job of carrying out their objectives. This group has done much to alert citizens to threats in the form of proposed laws that would tend to despoil the remaining natural beauty of the roadsides and has, in fact, fostered legislation to implement the work of rehabilitation. These and similar programs in the various states need the understanding and support of all interested citizens.

The character of a community and the people who live in it is clearly expressed by the condition of the approaches to the community. If the approach is good we expect to find

127

substantial, self-respecting people in residence there. If it is bad we know not what to expect but probably the worst.

Roadside rehabilitation and beautification begins with the simple task of good municipal housekeeping, the cleaning up of litter, collecting and disposing of all sorts of abandoned junk, clearing up unkempt roadside growth of weeds and weedy bushes, the removal of decrepit signs and buildings. This activity applies within a community as well as on its approaches and a good, successful clean-up program within a town or village can well point the way toward its extension into the surrounding countryside.

Many of our cities and towns are often disgracefully dirty and untidy. Merchants put all sorts of trash into their backyards, hoping it will be out of sight, but all too often it is plainly visible from adjacent streets, highways, and parking lots. They may even sweep their litter into the street gutter, trusting that either nature or perhaps the highway department will remove it. It is a sad commentary on the United States that one of the most common criticisms by overseas visitors is that whereas they enjoy and appreciate the friendliness of Americans they are conscious of our dirty streets and the noisiness of our cities and towns. Decent pride alone should lead us to do a better job of community housekeeping.

At a recent conference of the "Keep America Beautiful" organization, Secretary of Commerce Luther B. Hodges said that while America is getting richer it is also getting messier. According to figures supplied by his department it costs the American taxpayer five million dollars annually just to clean up litter from highways and another three million to clean up our public camping grounds. This money might better be spent, one would think, in a program of education in the schools and elsewhere to make this work unnecessary.

In the hopes of restraining him most states post signs advising the passing motorist of a heavy fine for littering, but convictions under such a law are hard to get. The offender is far away before his offense is noticed and he leaves no evidence of his identity. States also provide litter baskets and bins at some turnouts where picnic tables are placed and elsewhere but these are not always emptied often enough and they spill over or animals get into them and scatter the mess.

During the horse and buggy days every town had its corps of "white wings" who kept the streets clean, but with the advent of motor traffic these men seemed unnecessary. Motorized street sweepers have taken the place of the man with the broom, but not every community has equipped itself with these and those that have them do not always use them as often as they should. Of course, they are hampered by the multitude of cars parked along the streets of our communities.

In most communities, unfortunately, the local sanitation system is not set up to deal with anything more bulky than household garbage and trash. If anything larger needs to be disposed of, the householder must arrange for it himself. He often does not know where to take the thing, or has no means of transportation, or if he does know where the town dump is, he finds that it is so far away that he hesitates to make the trip. As a result he finds, instead, a convenient stretch of uninhabited roadside and leaves his discarded bedspring, mattress, sofa, refrigerator, or perhaps even his jalopy there!

Often the community lacks the money or the facilities to undertake the removal of this roadside trash and it may remain for months, meanwhile attracting other deposits of similar material and, suddenly, there is an unofficial dump right in the middle of what was a beautiful scene. This is a fast-growing problem in many a suburban area because the newcomers are not familiar with local conditions, and expect such services as trash removal to be available. On a recent flight to one of our large cities we could not help notice, as the plane lowered for a landing, the large accumulations of discarded junk of all sorts in the woods and along the roads near the airport. Because it was winter and the trees were bare of leaves these eyesores stood out in all their ugliness.

Much credit should be given to the various garden clubs and their National Council for their litterbug campaign which has spread rapidly and done much to bring forceably to people's attention the importance of not littering our streets and highways. "Litterbug" is now a derogatory epithet. They have advocated that every automobile carry a litter bag that can be emptied at home or at gas stations. In fact they have also been instrumental in seeing that trash baskets are placed in areas where trash is likely to originate. These are very necessary steps in the right direction because out in the country motorists are the greatest source of roadside litter. Today, when so many things come in disposable packages or in nonreturnable bottles, the problem is increasing. One wonders how many millions of disposable tissues have found a final resting place impaled on a twig alongside our roadways.

Advertising Signs and Billboards

Advertising signs in our towns and villages and billboards along our principal highways do much to mar civic beauty. Although identification by signs of reasonable size is necessary for retail shops and other similar businesses, when they become so numerous that they obscure or cancel each other, their value as advertising is largely wasted. Businessmen should realize this and, if for no other reason, resist the blandishments of sign salesmen who urge them to install bigger and flashier signs to outdo their neighbors.

Moving, flashing illuminated signs or those that flutter in the wind have no place in a well-managed community because they contribute excessively to clutter and ugliness.

Every community should have an ordinance governing the size, placement, and other pertinent details of signs either as a part of its zoning ordinance or as a separate by-law. Control of this aspect of community life is well within the power of the municipality. All it needs is a realization of the problem, a well-written ordinance, and proper enforcement to see that it is observed.

That the American public continues to tolerate the abuse of the countryside by the billboard industry is one of the great mysteries. Nothing detracts so much from the beauty of our remarkable highway system as the ubiquitous billboard. Perhaps because many people have become accustomed to them these signs are not noticed. If so their value as advertising must approach zero. It may be that our deference to the traditional American system of free enterprise and inviolable property rights deters many people from taking action against them.

Outdoor advertising is big business in America and supports powerful lobbies in all state legislatures and in the halls of Congress as well. No sooner is a proposal made to eliminate or curb billboards than these lobbies go into action; so far they have been remarkably successful in defeating legislation that would limit their activities. Nevertheless some progress has been made toward reducing this flamboyant scourge and much more is possible if the citizenry can be alerted to the dangers in such signs. In this field we need more restrictive legislation and stronger protests to the heads of the companies using this advertising medium.

The chief contributors to the billboard menace are reputable national advertisers. It is interesting to note that in states where a concerted effort by the interested public has produced a flood of letters of protest, the sale of billboard space has been reduced. In 1962, for example, fifty-three of the top one hundred national advertisers who had used billboard space in 1961 spent no money for outdoor advertising.

The beer and liquor advertising billboards represented only 8 per cent of the list as compared with 35 per cent in 1959. Perhaps this form of cooperation from advertisers will continue to aid the cause of beautification along our main highways. But this will only be true if the public supports the project.

It is possible to control billboard advertising within our municipalities through strict zoning and sign control ordinances, but in the outlying areas and the open countryside such ordinances seldom exist nor would they be practicable. More generalized and extensive legislation is necessary. When, in 1958, the Congress enacted legislation establishing the Federal Interstate Highway System, some controls over billboards adjacent to the new highways were written into the law. Stronger controls were defeated because terrific pressure against such regulations was brought to bear by the billboard industry. Unfortunately those supporting such regulations, the "Keep America Beautiful" organization, State Garden Clubs and others, were not strong enough. This clearly indicates that if the fight against billboards is to be won, there is a need for greater support from other organizations and from the general public. Constant vigilance is necessary against the tactics of the powerful billboard lobby if, before it is too late, the beauty of our countryside is to be saved.

Opposition to billboard control comes not only from the billboard industry itself but also from property owners along the right of way of a highway, aided and abetted, no doubt, by the billboard lobby. To the property owner the creation of a new highway through or along his property presents him with an unexpected (and unearned) bonanza—the opportunity to rent sites for billboards. This potential value is something the property owner hates to give up. But since this potential value has been created by the construction of the highway and is not inherent in the land as such, to deny the owner the right to capitalize on this new opportunity for profit is not depriving him of any right he ever enjoyed.

Even though a property owner may desire to rent space for a billboard along an existing, instead of a new, highway the question arises as to whose property he is actually using. He may own the site but if it is to be effective the billboard must be seen across other properties. Are these owners' rights being invaded? The question of air rights has not been fully explored by the courts but it has been established that an owner does not necessarily have air rights over the land of a neighboring property. Presumably, in the case of a state-owned highway, barriers of planting could be erected to hide such billboards but why should the state have to go to this expense? It is far simpler to pass legislation to ban any and all billboards that deface scenic beauty.

As this is being written a case that will no doubt become celebrated, and may establish a precedent, is moving through the courts in New York. It concerns the right of an abutting property owner, in this case a large grocery concern, to maintain a large, garish electric sign overlooking a portion of the New York World's Fair grounds. Robert Moses, a most ardent fighter for a cause he considers right, contends that the Fair organization has a right to block out this sign by the erection of what has been called a "spite fence" on the Fair grounds.

Nor are we entirely concerned with scenic beauty in our fight against billboards, important though it may be. Survey after survey prove that billboards along heavily traveled highways, or on less heavily traveled but narrow and crooked ones, are contributing causes of accidents. Where vision is restricted by a billboard, or where the message thereon is so arresting as to distract the driver's attention from his proper business of driving, the danger is intensified. If billboards are allowed to be placed near necessary caution or directional markers, by confusing the scene with extraneous items they render such important signs ineffective. Particularly bright-colored or moving signs are especially inappropriate in such a situation. From a safety angle alone, therefore, billboards along highways should be done away with.

The federal legislation relating to billboards along the Interstate Highway System is a step, though a fairly weak one, in the right direction. To get any legislation in a democratic system of government compromises have to be made. Under a law known as USC 131 the Congress in 1958 established a set of standards and controls relating to billboards and signs along federally aided interstate highways. The law is quite complicated and a detailed description of all provisions cannot be undertaken here. For specific information one should get in touch with the Bureau of Public Roads, U. S. Dept. of Commerce, Washington, D.C.

The purpose of the law is to encourage the states to enact specific legislation in this field. It makes no attempt to impose controls at the federal level. If a state decides to participate in the program the federal government undertakes to increase the amount of federal aid for the construction of highways within the state by half of 1 per cent of the cost thereof. This seems like a rather small percentage but it is some incentive at least and about twenty states have so far joined in the program. States, unfortunately, are not compelled to participate and the only penalty for nonparticipation is the loss of this small percentage of the cost of the project.

If a state does decide to participate it must comply with certain definite standards of performance the federal government has established. The Congress declared it a national policy that "the erection and maintenance of outdoor advertising signs, displays, or devices within 660 feet of the edge of the right of way, and visible from the main traveled way of all portions of the Interstate System constructed upon any part of the right of way the entire width of which is acquired subsequent to July 1, 1956, should be regulated consistent with natural standards to be prepared and promulgated by the Secretary [of Commerce]."

Careful reading of this statement will reveal that the program is quite limited in scope. It does not apply to those highways built on rights of way obtained, even in small part, prior to July 1, 1956, nor to signs further back from the highway than 660 feet. Nor does it apply to signs even within the proscribed distance but not visible from the interstate highway as might be the case at an intersection of the new road with an old, existing one. Nor does it apply, under an amendment adopted in 1959, to signs in industrial or commercially zoned areas within incorporated municipalities, or other areas where the land use as of September 21, 1959, was clearly established by state law as industrial or commercial.

Of course the states, on their own initiative, may further restrict outdoor advertising by including such areas within the controlled zones but they cannot thereby earn the half of 1 per cent of cost federal subsidy. Although the agreements entered into between the states and the federal government are statewide, payments provided for in the law will be paid on a project by project basis with respect to all projects or parts of projects to which the national policy is applicable. Federal participation on the half of 1 per cent of cost basis does not extend, either, to the acquisition of advertising rights which is a device sometimes resorted to for the purpose of eliminating signs, but, on rather a complicated basis, federal funds from other sources are available for this purpose.

Four classes of signs are permitted within the controlled areas, namely (1) official signs maintained by public officers (directional, mileage, caution, speed signs, and the like); (2) on-premise signs advertising activities being conducted on the property where the sign is located (signs on business establishments); (3) signs offering the property on which they stand for sale or rental; (4) signs in the specific interest of the traveling public (historic markers and signs relating to outdoor recreation, places for camping and lodging, food and vehicle service; lodging, food, and vehicle signs, however, must be within twelve miles of the place advertised). All these categories of signs are subject to specific regulations as to placement, size, distance from each other and from intersections, and the like.

This program of sign control applies, of course, only to a limited amount of federally aided highway construction and not at all to older national, state, county, or local highways, nor to new ones built without federal aid. It should, however, point the way toward more state and local legislation in this field. Kentucky was one of the first, if not the first state, to qualify for the half of 1 per cent of cost incentive money. Unfortunately the billboard lobbyists have blocked enabling legislation in some thirty states by succeeding in putting through crippling amendments.

Admittedly there have to be some signs on highways other than the federally controlled ones if we are going to get to our destination, obtain needed supplies and shelter, or find out something about the country through which we are passing. Such signs, however, do not need to be billboards. The federal program is perhaps a bit liberal in what it permits, especially regarding signs advertising something as much as twelve miles away, or failing to control on-premise signs as much as it might.

In controlling signs size alone should not be the criterion of excellence. Design and color are even more important. The directional signs put in place by the highway departments are generally admirable and the colors pleasing. Control signs, speed signs, and so on are fairly standardized throughout the nation, though one could put in a plea for the greater use of the pictorial signs seen all over Europe.

One need not be able to read to understand them and they have a certain charm of their own which adds to the enjoyment of travel.

Bad as the large billboards of national advertisers are, smaller, local signs are hardly less objectionable for there are so many of them that they often become confusing. Then, too, most of these are badly designed, badly placed, and often not well maintained. Tourism is getting to be "big business" in most states and unless there is more control of even these smaller, local signs much of the charm of the countryside for the traveler will be destroyed.

Today with excellent road maps available free at all service stations, the booklets and lists of approved or inspected motels and restaurants (also free for the asking), together with the wealth of informative material put out by the various state and local Chambers of Commerce, there is less reason than formerly for the many signs that tout local places for eating, sleeping, sight-seeing, and the purchase of gifts. Those signs calling attention to local, homemade or home-grown products we will have to learn to live with, but even here local interested groups might suggest improvements in design, placement, and upkeep even if complete control is out of the question.

A suggestion that might prove most helpful to the traveling public, and to local businesses as well, is to have every state and important cities and towns establish, maintain, and staff an information booth near their borders during the tourist season where pertinent information and correct directions can be obtained. Such information service was established when the Blue Ridge Highway and the Skyline Drive were opened and it has proved a success both to the traveler and those catering to the public even though their places of business are off the highway. It has permitted the elimination of all business signs along these highways.

Failing the establishment of an information service booth,

an alternative could be the erection of a well-designed sign or signs, well placed and planted so that the traveler could pull off the traveled way and read. Most travelers would not only like to know the name of the town through which they are about to pass but something of interest, historic notes, if any, principal industries, etc. Such signs should be brief and factual. They could also include the names of hotels, motels, restaurants, churches, service clubs, and the like. Pinehurst, North Carolina, has done an excellent job in this respect.

Roadside Commercial Clutter

One of the most important contributing factors to roadside ugliness is the uncontrolled commercial development that has been permitted to grow up along the highways leading in and out of our communities. It is everywhere and hardly a single village, however small, has escaped at least a touch of it.

Where zoning controls have not been imposed this sort of development has run wild. All sorts of inharmonious uses from hot-dog stands to funeral parlors spring up along the highway. Many of the older zoning ordinances actually encouraged this sort of development by placing in a commercial district strips of land only one hundred feet deep all along such highways. It was then thought that all business buildings would, of course, be built flush with the highway boundary and that therefore a depth of one hundred feet for a plot of ground on which to build would be ample. As conditions changed it was found that this sort of zoning was destructive to community appearance and property values as well. But by that time the damage had often been done and it was found difficult to correct it.

In fact one of the most baffling problems facing most communities today is how to get rid of undesirable commercial development in their outskirts. By proper zoning it is easy enough to prevent further expansion of this sort of thing, but how to get rid of, or at least clean up, organize, and improve the appearance of what we have is more difficult.

We probably can never get rid of roadside commercial development entirely. A large public demands the sort of convenient service it supplies and is largely indifferent to how it looks. Only a minority of the population is offended by the blatant commercialism in all its diverse forms.

Zoning controls carefully written not only to prevent further expansion of ugly commercial development along outlying highways but also to provide for limited land coverage, on-site parking, and sign control should certainly be enacted. Campaigns like clean-up, spruce-up, paint-up drives are temporarily effective but must be often repeated. Contests offering prizes for achievement in design of new or rehabilitation of older structures have their value. Awakening the community to an awareness of its appearance, and stimulating a will to do something about it, is something to which many a garden club or other organization could well devote its energies.

Automobile Graveyards and Junk Yards

One of the greatest blights on our American landscape is the prevalence of junk yards and automobile graveyards. In some of our most beautiful and picturesque areas they frequently desecrate roadsides and are even displayed on whole hillsides. Undoubtedly these things are, at present, a necessary evil but surely something can be done to make them less obvious, or to place them in less frequented or visible areas.

The vast waste of salvageable material is appalling to anyone coming from a country less affluent and less wasteful than ours and foreigners find it hard to understand how and why we permit it. Unfortunately we are such a spendthrift nation still believing that our natural resources are unlimited and that we do not need to salvage anything. The price of scrap metal, for example, is so low that the junk dealers absolutely refuse to become encumbered with old, worn-out automobiles.

These are generally stripped of certain movable parts having some slight resale value but the bulk of the chassis is left to be disposed of. Where? That is an excellent question but apparently it has no answer. The sanitation department, either public or private, will have nothing to do with these. The town dump or the incinerator refuses them. The only answer seems to be that one must pay to have them towed away to some convenient hill or roadside to become an eyesore to the whole community and the passing public, or, in the dark of night, deposit them along some rural road or in a vacant area, provided that all distinguishing marks that could be used to trace the owner have been removed. Terrible as this sounds it is becoming a far too frequent practice and an answer must be found by the municipal authorities.

We read with pride the statistics on automobile and appliance production. Our economic growth is amazing but for every new car or appliance sold there is, more often than not, an old one to be scrapped. Last year's car, turned in, is sold as a "used car." The buyer of this turns his car in on the transaction and it becomes a "second-hand" car. The next time it changes hands it becomes a "jalopy," and finally it is junked. The problem of disposing of all this worn out material is gigantic. We hear a great deal about the manufacture of "durable goods" but it is becoming apparent that the automobile, the washing machine, and the refrigerator are not among the durable things since they either go out of style or out of order at such a rate that we are not able to deal with their remains in a graceful manner.

Some forward-looking communities have purchased their own presses to process this junk material and so be able to handle it and sell it to scrap-metal dealers who will take it in this compacted style. This operation cannot be expected to operate at very much of a profit but at least it gets rid of the accumulation of unwanted material. Every large community should undertake such a program and the smaller ones should get together on a cooperative venture. Meanwhile steps must be taken to collect, confine, and hide this material as well as possible.

Zoning ordinances may contain provisions restricting the location of, and require the fencing or screening of, areas where such junk is stored. They may require that these yards be located in specific, remote areas and in places that cannot readily be seen. Sometimes junk material can be dumped into a ravine, swamp, or abandoned sandpit that will later be filled and probably never be built over because such material does not provide a very stable foundation.

One suggestion that may at first seem fantastic, but that might work well in some localities, is to load the old automobiles onto barges, tow them to deep water off shore, and dump them there. It is claimed they would create attractive places for fish to congregate to the delight of fishermen. Of course permission would have to be obtained from the federal government before any such program can be undertaken, and an area designated that would never interfere with navigation.

Public Dumps and Incinerators

Public dumps and incinerators are another distasteful community problem. Their location, appearance, and maintenance can have a profound effect on civic beauty. Frequently, in small towns and villages, these unsightly adjuncts come into being rather by accident than by design. Someone starts dumping in a field or patch of woodland convenient to the highway, the accumulation grows, and the municipality in self-defense finally buys the site and takes over the management. Unfortunately many of these casually located dumps prove to be in the wrong place entirely as far as community appearance is concerned. And many a community has had to destroy and move its improperly located incinerator because of public discontent over increasing odor, smoke, and the presence of obnoxious insects and rodents.

To find an acceptable site for these facilities within the municipal boundaries is always difficult and sometimes impossible. Nobody wishes to have them in his own particular neighborhood. Many communities resort to the device of buying or renting a site in an adjoining small community that is indifferent to the presence of a dump or incinerator in its sparsely settled confines. When this is done the intruding community has a responsibility to the one intruded upon, whether or not the victim realizes it, to maintain these facilities in a decent shape, to screen them, and to mitigate such nuisances as odor, smoke, and vermin.

Modern incinerators do not require the tall chimneys formerly found necessary for proper combustion and they pretty well control and eliminate smoke and odor. They are therefore less conspicuous than they used to be. One way to help promote civic beauty is to insist that the incinerator in the community be modernized along these lines. It can be housed in an attractive building, the grounds well maintained and attractively planted. Well-designed screen plantings can do a great deal to diminish the adverse effect of an incinerator on a neighborhood.

Open dumps and their attendant smoldering fires are certainly not to be recommended, but they are still frequently found throughout the country. Modern methods of sanitary land fill, if constantly pursued, can eliminate most, if not all, of the objectionable features of an open dump. If garbage, trash, and junk of any sort is promptly sprayed to eliminate insects and rodents and then immediately covered with clean fill, the result will ultimately be a piece of land that can be safely and profitably built on for commercial, industrial, or recreational purposes. The writers once constructed a large playground in a crowded urban situation on what had been the public dump, with good results. The New York World's Fair site in Flushing Meadows was, not too long ago, an immense New York City dump which was leveled and covered with good soil to permit the construction of not only the first World's Fair in 1939 and its planting, but the site then became a city park and is now being used again for the World's Fair of 1964. On and around this site an important series of highways have been built, indicating that properly filled dumps can become valuable property.

Roadside Care

One of the jobs that confronts every highway superintendent is the maintenance of the roadside verges in an acceptable condition. This means that they should remain covered with low verdure but that brush and young trees that might grow over the highway and impede traffic when bent with snow and ice, or which might grow tall enough to interfere with the overhead utility wires, be in some way controlled. Not all highway maintenance people realize the need to keep the roadsides green, despite state-erected signs to that effect, and a number of detrimental practices have been engaged in, together with some wise ones. The problem is to evaluate these, recommend and support the good ones, and oppose vigorously the detrimental ones.

It has been pretty well established that mowing the roadsides is not the best way to handle the problem unless the verges are only covered with grasses and other herbaceous plants and the area is flat enough to permit the safe traverse of the mowing machine. In such instances mowing in late summer or early fall is probably the wisest procedure. This does destroy the fall blooming plants—the asters and goldenrod—but the earlier blooming ones are spared. The tendency, especially along parkways, to mow repeatedly throughout the summer season is little less than disastrous because during the hot, dry periods the grass becomes completely brown and unsightly. Less mowing during these periods, or setting the blades of the mowing machines higher, would mitigate this condition.

Where the roadsides are steep or cluttered with rocks and other obstructions mowing can be a hazardous and expensive operation. Where brush, rather than grass, has to be mown the results are far from permanent. In fact repeated mowing of many species of seedling hardwood trees may merely aggravate the problem because the more these are cut the more numerous the resulting sprouts.

Roadside Spraying

The indiscriminate use of herbicide sprays to destroy brush and sprouting trees has produced deplorable results in many areas and given the whole program a bad reputation among conservationists and lovers of nature. Sprays, however, have proved in the long run to be both more effective and cheaper than mowing. The first year they are used the cost is considerably greater than a single annual mowing, but sprays are effective for five years or so, except in unusual situations, so the cost may be prorated over a longer period. Even then renewal sprays can be done, when necessary, on a spot basis.

This may appear to be making out a clear case in favor of roadside spraying, but this we have no intention of doing. As it has been handled in the past, and is even now being conducted, it is a little less than disastrous. In many rural areas instead of lush green we have roadside "brownout." It is not necessarily the fault of the sprays but is generally the careless, ignorant use of them that has caused the trouble.

Since Rachel Carson's *Silent Spring* was published, thousands of people have become aware of the dangers of indiscriminate use of either insecticides, fungicides, or herbicides. We have been thoroughly scared and it is to be hoped that we will remain scared enough to use these materials, if at all, with the greatest care. They are all dangerous and should be treated with great respect. They should never be entrusted to ignorant, indifferent, or careless hands.

As Miss Carson says, the blanket spraying of our roadsides with chemical herbicides to control roadside vegetation is turning our roads into barren, unsightly wastes. The state where these writers spend considerable time likes to call itself "the prettiest state" but it won't be if the authorities continue the current practices of roadside maintenance. This state, like many others, depends heavily for its income on the tourist, but if it allows itself to become unattractive this business will go elsewhere. Natural beauty depends not only on the distant views of mountains, lakes, and the sea, but also on the wildflowers, shrubs, and trees that deck our roadsides.

If blanket sprays cannot be tolerated because of the great damage they do, how is the spraying problem to be handled? Apparently selective sprays and selective spraying are the answers. Only those materials that kill the particular species it is intended to get rid of should be used. The thorough training of the spray crew is most important. Many of the cases of indiscriminate spraying or poor results can be traced to poorly trained crews or those who did not follow explicit directions. These men must know the different plant species both when in leaf and when dormant, and know which should be sprayed and which should be left alone. It is most important that low-growing ground-cover species, both herbaceous and woody, be encouraged to grow rather than be killed off not only because of the appearance of the roadside but also to prevent soil erosion.

The Northeastern Forest Experiment Station at Upper Darby, Pennsylvania, has found, after exhaustive study over several years of practical demonstration, that only the low-volatile esters of 2-4-5 T should be used. They do not recommend the use of 2-4 D mixed with 2-4-5 T. While this material (2-4-5 T) can be used in a water solution, better results were obtained when it was used with diesel oil.

Spraying can be done from trucks or from knapsack spray pumps carried by individuals. In those areas where it is highly desirable to avoid a blanket spray the individual knapsack in the hands of a well-trained crew member is, without doubt, the best method of operation though, of course, more expensive.

Usually a width of from six to eight feet from the traveled way is a sufficient area to cover, but on curves or at intersections a greater width may be necessary to maintain sight lines. Spraying can be done at any time when the ground is bare of snow and ice, but it is important that if it is to be done in summer the dying brush be cut and cleaned up immediately. If the spraying is done when the plants are dormant this cleanup can be delayed somewhat, but it should never be omitted. A large part of the criticism of roadside spraying comes from the appearance of sprayed roadsides that have not been cleaned up. Dead brush does not fall down and disappear promptly enough to permit nature to deal with it. Furthermore, much justified criticism has been leveled at the foliage spray method, which is easier to do but not nearly as efficient as the selective basal method. In the latter method the brush is cut and removed before the drenching spray is applied to stumps, stubs, and root areas.

By the use of selective sprays for two or three seasons the condition of growth along the highway will become stabilized, perhaps for years, without further treatment and the low-growing material which has been spared will not only continue to clothe the roadsides with verdure but will also discourage the germination of seeds from less desirable trees and shrubs. Selective spraying uses less spray material and hence is cheaper than the blanket spray, to say nothing of appearances. It is also a sound conservation measure. Unobnoxious plants are preserved and, to a degree, protected so that the countryside remains beautiful and interesting.

Dr. Frank Egler and a group of associated ecologists and botanists have recently formed an association known as Right-of-Way Resources of America and great credit is due them, as well as the Northeastern Forest Experiment Station, for their pioneer work in developing an ecologically sound program of selective spraying. Dr. Egler's headquarters are at Falls Village, Connecticut. The Connecticut Arboretum, Connecticut College, New London, has prepared a bulletin, No. 13, on "What Is Happening Along Our Roadsides." This should be in the hands of everyone concerned with a roadside spraying project.

Roadside Planting

Having mentioned several of the things that create ugliness along our highways, the negative side, we must now consider several things, on the positive side, that will help make these highways more attractive and interesting. When one realizes how uninteresting most of our roadsides are, especially along the newer highways, one's first thought is, "Let's plant something." This is a good impulse and should be encouraged. Regrettably, however, much of the work undertaken in response to this idea has proved to be futile because of the very impulsiveness under which it was undertaken. Someone has called this "impulsive ignorance" and we must caution against starting any civic program of this sort without first obtaining the cooperation and support of the authorities having jurisdiction over the area to be planted or otherwise improved and being sure of adequate financing. We do not intend to apply the brakes to anyone's enthusiasm toward creating improvement in our surroundings, but we hope our warning will help to avoid disappointment and failure.

One of the greatest disadvantages in living near, or facing on, a superhighway or other heavily traveled road is the noise generated by the constantly moving traffic. At a distance this may sound much like the ocean surf and is not unpleasant. Close to, however, it can be nerve-wracking and very difficult to become accustomed to. Some people quickly become inured to it and hardly hear it but others find it a constant irritation. Not much can be done to eliminate the noise, present-day vehicles being what they are, but if an adequate screen planting can be installed along the highway its effect can be greatly diminished. The United States Bureau of Public Roads states that if proper planting is installed the noise may be reduced by at least one half, that is, from about seventy decibels to around thirty. Where the highway is on the level with adjoining property the planting barrier needs to be thicker and higher than when the highway is depressed. When the highway is elevated the noise seems to flow over the immediate vicinity and is often more noticeable at a considerable distance. In such a situation, unless really massive planting is installed close to the traveled highway right of way, little improvement can be expected to result from it.

Such screen plantings do as much, if not more, for the highway itself because they shut off distracting and ugly views such as the rear portions of abutting properties which are not always as attractive as they might be, thus creating a more parklike atmosphere. Many consider a highway, especially the newer superhighways, as nothing more than a quick means of getting from one point to another, but there is no reason why these roads cannot be properly planted, graded, and in every other particular designed so that they are beautiful as well as useful. Today when our massive road building program covers every state we should not only realize how many thousands of acres of open space are being used up, but also how many countless acres are being opened up to view for the first time. We must strive to create as much beauty as possible rather than content ourselves with mile after mile of ugly scars across the country resulting from modern road building.

Whenever the climate and the soil permit, roadside screen plantings should contain both deciduous and evergreen trees. These should be interspersed with and edged down by shrub plantings to provide density enough to deflect sound waves moving along the ground. Native species rather than the more horticultural or gardenesque types should be chosen not only because they are likely to get rather less than expert care, which the native sorts can be content with, but without which the more exotic types cannot prosper, but partly because the native varieties will give a desirable regional character to those sections of the highway where they are used. In the East flowering dogwood, flowering crab apples, and hawthorns interspersed with various pines can be most effective. In the Middle West the hawthorns also do well as do most apples, horse chestnuts, many oaks, pines, and junipers. In the South the list is long and rich containing the hollies, yaupons, and evergreen oaks which provide a distinctive regional flavor. In the mountain areas of the West many cedars, firs, and spruces along with deciduous small trees and shrubs can be used effectively, and in the coastal regions other native species can lend a very distinct regional aspect to the plantings that will prove to be of especial interest to the tourist.

By the careful use of foliage color, texture, and form of

trees and shrubs, pleasing compositions can be created that are far more attractive than haphazard planting or mere reforestation. Because of its fleeting character the color of blossoms, though interesting, is not as important as the color of foliage, texture, and the shape of plants. Furthermore, individual flowers or flowering groups cannot be adequately studied and appreciated from an automobile moving at sixty miles an hour or faster.

Wherever the right of way is wide enough individual specimen trees or large shrubs can be used to provide desirable variety and interest. Many evergreen conifers which cannot be used as street trees are especially beautiful when they stand alone in an open area where they can grow in their natural, symmetrical manner. Such plants must, of course, be placed far enough back from the traveled way so that they do not have to be mutilated as they grow to avoid interference with traffic. Highway people dislike having the shadow of trees across the roadway. In the colder sections such shadows may cause icing in winter, or may be confusing to drivers but we feel that providing alternating shadow and sunlight along the highway, even a superhighway or expressway, would be one good way of reducing the monotony characterizing such highways and would greatly reduce eye fatigue.

Heavy screen plantings along highways can also serve effectively as snow breaks. If placed at the right distance from the pavement snow is deposited in drifts before it reaches the traveled way. The use of planting instead of portable snow fence that must be put in place and then taken down every year improves the appearance and lowers maintenance costs. According to an Ohio State Highway engineer, mass planting can also be used effectively to accent the curvature in highways to make night driving safer. Roadside plantings also help prevent soil erosion, especially on long, steep slopes where cuts have been made, and provide food and shelter for wildlife. Most important of all they beautify the roadside.

The median strip on most of the new highways offers great opportunities for proper landscape treatment and should be given much greater attention. Where the strip is very narrow, as it must be when roads go through areas of high land values, a metal divider is often installed for safety. Effective as these are in preventing head-on collisions they are ugly indeed. Wherever possible a hedge should be planted either side of them to hide their distressing appearance. These will at the same time cut off much of the headlight glare of oncoming traffic.

Where the median strip is wider, crash barriers of shrub plantings may be used. When fairly low-growing twiggy plants are used such barriers will stop a car going fifty miles an hour without injuring the occupants though the car's paint may be quite badly scratched by the impact. Where the median strip is much wider it is often graded to carry off storm water. It cannot be so heavily planted as to hamper the flow of water but groups of shrubs and small trees can be arranged to add to the attractiveness of the area and help provide shields against oncoming headlights. As every cross-country driver knows, such plantings are particularly necessary on curves. Even when the road edge is painted with luminous paint, which of course it should be, a driver is often temporarily blinded by oncoming lights in the opposite roadway.

If the median strip and the side areas along roads are maintained in grass they must be mowed at least several times a year. This is expensive and, if the side areas are steep, hazardous. If, on the other hand, these areas are more heavily planted with trees, shrubs, and ground covers, depending on the situation, the cost of maintenance is reduced and the highway beautified as well. There is nothing very attractive about unkempt grass areas and when closely mown they burn an unpleasant brown during prolonged hot, dry spells in summer.

As anyone who has driven long distances on the new superhighways knows, the road unwinding mile after mile exerts a decidedly hypnotic effect. This is especially true when the road passes through uninteresting country and where there is a paucity of roadside planting to attract interest. Any legitimate opportunity to break up this monotony must be taken advantage of, if only for safety's sake. Among the most obvious places to do this are the various interchanges, where bridges cross the highway and have high abutments, or where the roadway has been cut through a hillside. Many of these areas can be made attractive by judicious planting without in any way interfering with sight lines for traffic. These plantings become significant breaks in the long, monotonous ribbon of roadway.

Plant material for use in these areas should be carefully chosen, mainly for such plant characteristics as color of foliage, texture, and the form of the plants themselves. Vines, which can hardly be used elsewhere along a main highway, can be used effectively to clothe very steep banks and bridge abutments. Low evergreens and sprawling plants can be massed on slopes, and high-branched trees can be used to accent these compositions, giving them a significant third dimension. The use of vines and low-growing, twiggy material as ground covers also helps check erosion. In shady areas low herbaceous plants like ferns and other native species can be used largely because they avoid serious maintenance problems.

One of the most serious lacks along the new superhighways, and many of the older parkways, is a sufficient number of places to pull off the road and stop for a rest. So many of these fast traffic roads have signs telling the motorist he must maintain a minimum speed of at least 40 m.p.h. and that he can stop only for emergency repairs. The very occasional sign "Roadside Rest Ahead" is often most welcome, but when the motorist arrives there only too often he finds merely an inadequate turnout and nothing else. We have mentioned elsewhere that these stopping places need to be of adequate size and be equipped with at least a few facilities. We have not stressed, however, that they present a unique opportunity to do some effective roadside beautification.

Since people will stop at these places and often get out of their cars, the use of greater detail and intricacy in planting is permissible. Here is where really studied compositions of plants of all sorts can be arranged without the danger that they will not be appreciated as would be the case where traffic is moving too fast to observe such detail. These rest areas should not be considered by the highway engineers as luxuries but something of fundamental importance to the success of the whole project. The federal government has barred service areas from the new interstate highways but this should not mean that no rest areas of any sort should be provided.

In fact they should be created at quite frequent intervals, but whenever possible the sites should be selected to be interesting in themselves. Perhaps a shady ravine near a small stream, pond, or lake, or just a grove of fine old trees can help make the spot distinctive. Once selected the area should be carefully developed. To begin with it needs ample parking space. Many so-called rest areas are far too small. Picnic tables and benches, even a fireplace, if the area is one in which outdoor fires can be permitted with safety, should be provided. Drinking water should be available if at all possible, and toilet facilities, but these must be kept clean and neat. If this sort of maintenance cannot be counted on it is wiser to omit them, but if there are to be no service areas they will have to be provided for the traveling public.

Opportunities for the development of similar rest areas

along older highways exist when a curve is eliminated, or when for other reasons the alignment of the road is changed, and far too often these are not taken advantage of. Some states have created attractive areas and made quite a feature of them. They are very welcome and necessary because people in greater numbers are taking to the road in good weather in the hope of finding some delightful spot to stop at to have a picnic meal. Too often they are frustrated in their search for such a place either because it does not exist or because others have got there first and pre-empted the limited facilities.

The question is often posed as to who should do this roadside planting and development work. Obviously the highway people should take care of the paving of turnoffs and equip them with permanent structures and utilities, and it is to be hoped that sufficient money is appropriated for at least basic planting with more to be put in place later if it is not possible to do an adequate job at once.

Garden clubs and roadside committees have frequently undertaken roadside beautification improvement projects; though these projects are praiseworthy they are often handicapped by inadequate financing. Nor should these groups be made responsible for paying for such work, much less shouldering the burden of future maintenance. Perhaps their most important role in roadside development and beautification is to serve as a goad to get projects formulated and money appropriated to carry them out.

If competent professional advice is not to be had in the highway engineer's office itself, the appropriation should of course cover its cost. The cost of the plants and planting might, if advisable, be divided between the public authorities and a private local group. Often the highway department furnishes the transportation and labor and the sponsoring group the plants. However it is done, it should be a cooperative effort and fully supported both officially and financially by the authority having jurisdiction over the site.

Sometimes local garden clubs or other organizations have been asked to foot the whole bill but this seems somewhat of an imposition on the part of the tax-supported highway authorities. Garden clubs are keenly interested in the development and beautification of our highways because they fully realize that the elimination of the ugly or the commonplace does much to improve our everyday environment. But few of these clubs have either sufficient funds to pay for this sort of thing, or the training and experience in landscape architecture to do it as it should be done.

Before passing on to other matters, tribute must be paid to the Blue Star Memorial Highway program instituted by the Federated Garden Clubs of New Jersey and later adopted as a project by the National Council of State Garden Clubs. Its objective was to plant trees in memory of the men and women who had defended the United States in World Wars I and II. This program is still alive and active and has accomplished much. It deserves universal support.

11. Local Planning and Zoning

Up to this point we have been discussing the various phases of civic beautification, development, and improvement in general terms, hoping to arouse interest and to point out those areas where the average citizen can act to bring about either official or group action toward making his home town a better and more beautiful place in which to live and work. Every move that is made, however, must be made within the framework of existing federal and state laws, or local by-laws or ordinances. However enthusiastic one may be, one may not happily embark on some project for civic beautification without finding out first under whose jurisdiction the project lies, within what legal restrictions it is enclosed, and whose cooperation must be obtained to ensure its success. It behooves anyone interested in or taking part in such a project to know what the governing regulations are.

In all fifty of these United States the legislatures, in whose hands all the power to enact and enforce the law lies, have from time to time, and in varying degrees, delegated some of their power to local municipal governments—cities, counties, villages, towns, special districts. Though the legislation is similar throughout the country, just how much power they have so delegated, and to what extent, varies from state to state. Since this is so it is wise, before embarking on any project, to familiarize one's self with the local applicable laws and ordinances. The state publishes its laws in book form and these can be obtained from the local or state library on loan. Local attorneys undoubtedly have copies of the state's statutes which can be made available. Many states also publish pamphlets and brochures dealing with such subjects as Planning and Zoning, Traffic Control, Recreational Facilities within the state, Conservation, and many others. The Secretary of State or Commisioner of Commerce at the state capital can give information about these.

Under the powers so delegated by the states to the local governments these have adopted numerous ordinances, local by-laws, and codes, and it is under them that most civic improvement projects will have to be undertaken. These local laws come into being in any one of several ways. The governing authority on its own initiative may enact them. Civic groups of one sort or another may bring pressure to bear for their adoption. Interested parties such as industrial corporations may lobby a favorable (to them) local ordinance through the local legislative body. In all these cases it is important that an alert citizenry remain constantly aware of what is being proposed in order that beneficial laws may be adequately supported and harmful proposals soundly defeated.

Most such ordinances are originally drafted by the local officials, a professional planning consultant, or by an attorney, either employed by the municipality or by some private individual or corporation that hopes to have the ordinance enacted. This is normal procedure but, and it is a big but, someone should scrutinize all laws and ordinances that may have a bearing on the future development of the community, its appearance and other amenities to see that these aspects of the situation have neither been overlooked nor threatened by the proposed legislation. Every garden club or other organization interested in civics should maintain a standing committee whose duty it is to read proposed legislation, attend public hearings on it, and report back to its own organization in time for that organization to take united action should it be deemed necessary. Only by this means can those laws that occasionally try to sneak through the local legislative body, to the detriment of the whole community and for the benefit of some favored few, be forestalled before enactment. It is much easier to prevent action than to repeal or correct it later on. It is also regrettable that some good proposals that may lack widespread support could have been achieved enactment if group and citizen support had been marshalled to their support in time.

Within the last few decades planning has become a firmly established part of municipal government. Of course not all communities have, as yet, set up planning boards, but a large number have and many others should, so as to protect themselves from unplanned growth and the many dangers of rapidly expanding suburbanism. Almost everyone today regards planning as necessary and it is generally believed that it can solve most, if not all, community problems. This is an overoptimistic attitude. Planning certainly is important but it is not a universal cure-all.

Unless he makes a special effort, the average citizen of a small town or suburb has little opportunity to come to know his planning board, or to find out how it operates. He may go to a public hearing, if he is fortunate enough to find out that one is being held, but there he is likely to find planning operating in a rather confused and bureaucratic manner. The public hearing often becomes of little significance or a place to air private grievances and to advance special interests rather than a place where a proposal may be calmly studied and intelligently evaluated. This is unfortunate. The only valid reasons for a public hearing are to provide an opportunity to inform the public of proposals affecting the community, and to make certain that the administration does not secretly put through proposals that favor some individual at the expense of others. This does not often happen but without the legal requirement that there be a public hearing on proposed legislation it easily could.

In almost every suburban community, and especially in many subdivisions, a civic association has been formed with the ostensible purpose of looking after the interests of the people in the community. In most of these organizations a committee has been set up that is supposed to keep track of community affairs and to inform the members of what the local government is proposing. Other organizations such as the various service clubs—Rotary, Kiwanis, Lions, etc.— should also have similar liaison officers who can obtain information about the activities of the various official bodies and pass it on to their members.

If time and interest permit it is wise for the ordinary citizen to visit the office of the local planning board occasionally, get to know the staff, and discuss informally the problems that are being worked on. In this way he will be able, at a hearing, to ask intelligent questions or propose sensible alternate solutions for a perplexing problem.

Planning boards are generally assumed to have an interest in all phases of community development, residential, recreational, cultural, commercial, and industrial. That some of them find themselves so burdened with the job of dealing with land subdivision maps that they cannot take time to think of much else, is unfortunate, but if an interested and enthusiastic group of citizens comes before them with a community project they are in duty bound to listen, to discuss the matter, and act on it (not necessarily favorably, of course). For citizens to approach their planning board intelligently and constructively, they should understand something of the background and operation of municipal planning as it is conducted in most communities. They should be familiar with the workings of the zoning ordinance and the Board of Zoning Appeals.

Of course many matters that come before a planning board are not susceptible of improvement on the part of untrained persons. They are technical and, as in the case of subdivisions, are controlled by so many legal, engineering, and economic factors that by the time they reach the public hearing stage they are pretty much in final form. Though they may appear to have many defects the planning board is probably well aware of these but has been unable, for one reason or another, to do anything to remove them. The insistence, for example, on the part of a developer that the proposed street layout of the subdivision yield the highest possible number of lots the zoning ordinance permits cannot easily be denied regardless of the fact that the proposed street system may produce some awkwardnesses, the destruction of fine trees, or more drastic alteration of the natural topography than is desirable. The trouble here lies with the basic ordinance, not with the planning board's operations under it.

Basic Enabling Legislation

When the need for municipal planning became evident, and had generated a considerable amount of citizen support, the legislatures of the various states enacted a group of laws enabling local municipalities to establish planning agencies and defined their duties and powers. Definite limitations were set to their authority and this is something that often frustrates not only the planning officials themselves but also the citizens who cannot see why, when a sensible-seeming proposal is made, the planning board cannot bring about its official adoption and execution.

The legislatures, however, in guarding the powers of the local village or town boards and city councils, made the planning group advisory only, with no power to compel action on any of its proposals, with one exception. In most states if the local municipal officials wish to do so, they may delegate to the planning board the power to pass on and approve plans for land subdivision. This is the only actual power the planning boards have. All else is advisory and action to implement any other type of decision must be taken by the village or town board, or the city council. The planning board may, and certainly should, make all sorts of suggestions, proposals, and recommendations to the governing body and urge their adoption, by every available means.

Zoning as a Tool in Planning

Many people think of zoning rather than planning as the more important phase of community development, but zoning is only one of many recognized tools in planning. It is not an end in itself, and is valuable only in so far as it furthers well-conceived and approved plans for the development and growth of the community. Frequently the zoning tail has been allowed to wag the planning dog, in fact, in many communities zoning has been instituted without accompanying it with a proper planning establishment—a long bushy tail but no dog. Unfortunately the legislation is often so worded that communities are permitted to approach this subject in this back-handed fashion. A village can have zoning without planning but, as we shall see, this hardly makes much sense.

The whole purpose of planning is to provide a continuing guiding principle to steer the community in the direction in which its citizens wish it to go. If, as is possible under many state statutes, a zoning commission is first appointed to produce a zoning map which the municipal government adopts, and is then disbanded, a one-shot deal results which tends to freeze the community in the pattern that exists at the moment, and which fails to provide any machinery for future revision, improvement, or progress. Where this procedure has been adopted a tendency develops to regard the zoning map as something final and immutable, more or less as a contract between the municipality and the property owner, which the municipality is obligated not to modify. The property owner, however, feels free to ask that it be modified if this appears to be in his private interest.

Much bitter controversy arises over this point. No community remains static. Conditions change. When this happens, and the municipal officials, individuals, or groups desire to amend the zoning map to meet new conditions, they are confronted with violent opposition. "You promised that if we went along with the original zoning proposal our neighborhood would remain one-family residential forever!" Sensible planning cannot operate in this manner. Zoning should never be regarded as permanent, nor should it ever assume contractual aspects.

Planning Should Precede Zoning

Let us, therefore, have planning before we attempt zoning, though not too much time should elapse between the establishment of a planning board and the enactment of a good zoning ordinance. The process should begin by the appointment, by the municipal authorities, of a planning board. In some states this is accomplished by popular election which, in the writers' opinion is less desirable, though both methods embody inherent dangers. Through political favoritism the wrong people can get appointed and, if they are good politicians, whether they know anything about planning, the wrong people can get elected. In a community that has adopted a watchful attitude toward its elected officials, the chances that good people will be appointed to the planning board are good. Since this group must work closely together it is important that they be congenial, which can be provided for when they are selected by appointment, but for which election makes no provision.

Where the problem is approached from the zoning rather than from the planning angle, the first step is the appointment of a zoning commission which prepares a zoning ordinance. When this has been duly adopted by the municipality the zoning commission ceases to function. Its members may be reappointed to constitute the first planning board, thus providing a certain amount of continuity, or an entirely new group may be selected.

Basic Studies

The first task before a newly appointed or elected planning board is to make a careful and thorough survey of the community to find out what its assets and potentialities are. Not until this is done can any sensible program of development be prepared. The community's illnesses and shortcomings cannot be prescribed for until one knows what ails it. Nor can its future be envisioned until one knows what it appears to be capable of achieving.

This work is arduous and time consuming, but it will prove to be time well spent. Many planning boards rush into the preparation of a zoning map and ordinance before they do anything else. Pressure is brought to bear on them to do this because of some threatened development the community does not want and which it fears will damage its future. Frequently the stimulus necessary to bring about the establishment of a planning board is sparked by just such a threat, and immediate action to deal with the problem is demanded. If this is the case the enactment of a temporary ordinance is wise. Get something on the books that will deal with the immediate threat, but so worded that complete revision can be accomplished when the necessary basic studies of the community have been completed. Stress its temporary character to forestall opposition to future revision and improvement.

These basic studies the planning board should make will consist of land-use maps, traffic counts and traffic maps, street and highway maps, park and recreation area maps, and statistics and information of all sorts about the various things that make up the community. Obviously this work will take considerable time, and at least a year should be allotted to it. In this field haste surely makes waste. If at all possible the planning board should be able to avail itself of the services of a planning technician who has been trained to collect and evaluate information pertinent to planning. The municipality should be prepared to provide in its budget funds to pay for an adequate, capable staff for the planning operation.

A land-use map will indicate what each and every parcel of land in the community is presently used for. Nothing else will so thoroughly familiarize a planning board with its community as the making of such a map, and we would suggest that, onerous though it may be, part of the work of gathering this information be done by the board members themselves rather than by their staff. It is difficult to see how a board can plan intelligently unless it knows its community thoroughly, and how better to gain this knowledge than through personal inspection.

Every planning board member should know where every street and alley in his community is. He ought to know where as many of the people live as possible since he is going to have to listen to them at public hearings and he will find this sort of information very useful in evaluating their remarks. He will know at first hand where the beauty spots in the community are and where the eyesores are located, where things are in pretty good shape and where something is needed to improve others. He will be able to tell what vacant areas seem appropriate for commercial, industrial, or residential development, and which should be put to other uses or saved from development. He will discover for himself where the awkwardnesses in the street pattern are and why traffic problems occur. And most important he will see and sense how the community goes about the business of daily living.

Plan of Development

With all this information at hand the planning board is ready to begin work on a plan for the development of the community. This can be a very sketchy affair, consisting of fragmentary maps and reports, or it can be a detailed and beautifully presented affair fit for framing. Its purpose is to give impetus and direction to the community's planning activities. In our opinion it should never become a strait jacket into which the community is forced by the legal adoption of a so-called Master Plan. The plan should be fluid and easy to change and improve. If a Master Plan is legally adopted and filed, changes become difficult and time consuming. The result is either that the plan is pigeon-holed somewhere in the municipal offices and forgotten or, if it is adhered to rigidly, the community is stultified. Of the two courses the former is, perhaps, the wiser choice, illegal though it sometimes may be.

This plan of development will consist of maps and reports indicating not only the proposed zoning districts, but the location of proposed parks and recreational facilities, buildings for municipal services, new and realigned highways, and anything else of present or future significance. Before this plan is approved, further public hearings should be held to give the citizens an opportunity to bring forth suggestions for regulations and projects that may not have been included, or to register their opposition or support for the things the report contains. This is the point at which the average citizen can function effectively. After all these ideas have been considered the plan should be approved by the governing body of the municipality. It will serve henceforth as a guide to the community's development. A plan of development which is merely approved but not legally adopted can be amended without difficulty and provides a desirable flexibility for the planning program. Of course it should not be construed that because the plan is so easy to amend it may be disregarded, but conditions change so rapidly in a fast-growing community that, in maintaining a planning program, flexibility is desirable.

Zoning Ordinance

Accompanying the approval of the development plan come the zoning map and ordinance, including regulations governing the subdivision of land and required public improvements. A building code, if the community lacks one, and quite possibly in a complex community a housing code, plumbing and sanitary code, electrical code, and a fire code will be needed. These are all useful planning tools, the first three being absolutely essential even in the smallest community—a development plan, a zoning setup, and subdivision regulations.

In many such ordinances and regulatory codes the consideration of community aesthetics and design is almost entirely absent. This is because such instruments, drawn up by lawyers, politicians, or engineers, have not been subjected to any scrutiny by persons knowledgeable in the aesthetic field. Every planning board should have among its members at least one person devoted to or skilled in the arts or the design professions. An artist, an architect, a landscape architect, or a member of a garden club must be there to bring to bear on all decisions his point of view which, surely, will be that the community should increasingly become more attractive and more beautiful and thus become a better place in which to live and work, as well as a more efficient operating entity. Practical considerations must not always be permitted to dominate the board's thinking. The amenities must have their share of attention.

With a board so constituted vast progress can be made, even under the present limited powers of these boards, to bring about improvements in the appearance of towns and villages, to fight ugliness, to eliminate eyesores, and to foster good design in buildings, good community housekeeping, the preservation of beautiful landscapes and historic sites, the saving of open space, the development of useful and attractive areas for recreation and relaxation and cultural activities of all sorts.

One of the mistakes communities frequently make when trying to adopt a zoning ordinance for the first time is to copy one from some neighboring community with what are referred to as "minor changes." This is usually done for the sake of expediency. It is easier to copy than originate. Almost always, however, such ordinances are not tailored closely enough to the peculiarities of the particular community in question. Every community differs from every other one, and no ordinance governing the use of private property can be expected to fit a wide variety of communities with their vastly differing desires, physical characteristics, and aspirations. Any such copied ordinance will run into difficulties of adoption and, even if it does get passed, it will create administrative problems one could well do without. Each community should have its own ordinance carefully designed to meet its special conditions and requirements.

An ordinance intended to be applied to a rapidly growing suburb would necessarily be long and quite detailed. There would have to be numerous zone districts each having its own set of regulations. On the other hand an ordinance for a more or less static village remote from a metropolitan area should be quite brief, with few zone districts and as few regulatory provisions as possible.

Zoning originated as a device for controlling the use, height, and bulk of buildings in the interest of health, safety, and general welfare, in other words under the police power. Every zoning ordinance therefore must be justified under one or more of these criteria. Does it promote health? safety? or general welfare? If not, it exceeds the police power and is probably unconstitutional. Thus matters that are clearly outside this area of authority should not be placed in a zoning ordinance. They will be struck down by the courts when and if they come before them. Nevertheless, as the courts have become increasingly liberal in their interpretation of the police power to encompass zoning provisions that had formerly been regarded as improper, more provisions aimed in purely aesthetic directions have been declared valid.

This is where civic beautification again enters the picture. A modern zoning ordinance may legally contain numerous provisions aimed at making the growing community a more beautiful one. Developers may be required to plant street trees of a specified size and variety. They may be required to provide extra-wide rights of way for streets so that grass verges between the property line and the curb can be wide enough to accommodate shrub and tree plantings. Decorative pylons with appropriate planting may be required at the entrance to a subdivision. Electric wiring may be required to be placed underground. Decorative street lighting is also possible. Small open spaces at street intersections, properly designed so as not to interfere with traffic sight lines, can be required and suitably planted. The setting aside of a reasonable percentage of land in a subdivision for a public park or playground may be required.

During the process of approval the layout of streets may be altered within reason by the planning board to produce more pleasing curves and grades. Steep banks and ugly fills may be prohibited. Where water catchment basins are required, the fencing and planting around them may be required to be attractive as well as useful. In commercial and industrial areas the ordinance may not only require the buildings to be low and widely spaced, but it may require the installation of lawns, screen plantings, and properly paved and screened parking areas. Off-street parking for all districts, including residential ones, may be required. All these things, once thought beyond the scope of a zoning ordinance, may now be incorporated in it with the result that from henceforth the appearance of the community will be greatly improved.

Procedures of Adoption

Every community must face the fact that the task of getting a zoning ordinance and its subdivision regulations approved and adopted by the municipality is not a quick or easy one. The fight will revolve around the fact that the zoning ordinance is (let's face it) an ordinance depriving private property of certain rights for the benefit of the community as a whole. Every American citizen resents having any of his rights taken away for any reason at all and, regardless of the fact that such an ordinance will benefit many, he will react unfavorably. He must be convinced first that the rights he is being deprived of are not necessary to his happiness or prosperity, or at least not very necessary, whereas the benefits to be derived by the community are important and permanent.

It should be remembered, and constantly stressed, that a development plan with its various necessary ordinances should be a live and vital thing—not a final solution of the community's problems once and for all time, but a working guide to a step-by-step solution. To solve all the community's problems at once is impossible and should not be attempted. We should move slowly, step by step, and remain always open to contrary suggestions and opinions. Always remain within the realm of the possible.

Board of Zoning Appeals or Board of Adjustment

Since no zoning ordinance can or should be so detailed that every possible situation in the community is prescribed for, every good ordinance provides for a Board of Appeals or a Board of Adjustment, as they are variously called. These boards are given specific powers under the ordinances to vary provisions when physical difficulty or unnecessary hardship would be occasioned by strict compliance; to interpret the ordinance and to determine the exact location of district boundaries; to grant special permits whenever the ordinance spells out what these are and under what circumstances they may be issued. These are the only powers these boards have, and they must be exercised strictly in accordance with the provisions of the ordinance.

Sometimes during the agitation that often accompanies the adoption of a zoning ordinance, people are led to believe that if a provision of the ordinance is disadvantageous to them, all they have to do is to appeal for a variance and it will be granted. This impression is often created purposely by the proponents of the ordinance in order to combat opposition to its adoption, but since it is not legally possible for a Board of Appeals to act in such a manner, it should never be restored to. The board's powers are strictly limited. It may not grant permits or variances in defiance of clearly expressed provisions of the ordinance nor, in effect, rewrite it to fit some peculiar set of circumstances. Some inexperienced boards have grossly exceeded their legal powers and have granted illegal permits and variances. If these ever get into court everybody is in trouble.

When a property owner finds that something he is planning to do would be contrary to the expressed provisions of the ordinance, he may apply for a variance. For example, an owner may propose to build on a lot that is so steep, so rocky, or covered with water to such an extent that he cannot locate his building within the required set-back limits. He may appeal for permission to modify these requirements. If the board is convinced that the practical difficulty or an unnecessary hardship really exists, it may grant a variance sufficient to permit the building to be erected. But it may not grant more than the minimum deviation from the terms of the ordinance necessary to accomplish this. It cannot set the ordinance aside entirely.

Variances are, therefore, limited to special physical obstacles to compliance with the ordinance. They do not extend to such matters as a change of use from a permitted to a prohibited one. For example, if a property owner wishes to conduct a business in a residential zone the Board of Appeals is powerless to permit him to do so. He must apply for and obtain a change of zoning to accomplish his desires. The power to make a zoning change rests in the town or village board, not in the Board of Appeals.

If, however, the ordinance clearly specifies certain uses as not permitted by right in a particular zoning district but sets forth certain standards to guide the Board of Appeals when considering applications for such uses, the board, if it makes an affirmative finding, can grant a special permit. These standards may contain provisions whose objective is civic beautification such as the requirement of street trees, screen planting, or off-street parking. This is the so-called special permit, or special exception power of the board, and is quite distinct from the power to grant variances. These two distinct powers are frequently confused in the public mind and are referred to loosely under all circumstances as variances. They are separate and distinct and this should be understood by the public, particularly by anyone attending a public hearing either to support or to oppose an appeal that may come before the board.

Applications to the Board of Appeals may be made by any property owner who feels that what he proposes to do cannot be accomplished in strict compliance with the ordinance, or who has been denied a building permit. Upon receipt of such an application the board advertises a public hearing which any citizen of the community may attend and at which he may be heard. Most ordinances provide that property owners within a specified distance from the property under consideration (usually 200 feet) shall be sent a copy of the notice of the hearing through the mails.

Citizens should be encouraged to attend Board of Appeals hearings not only so that they will become acquainted with proposals affecting them and their neighborhood, but also to make sure that the board is not acting capriciously or unfairly. Most boards take their job very seriously and would not intentionally act improperly, but some have been known to favor their friends at the expense of the community, and some are inexperienced and may act impulsively.

In fast-growing communities these boards are burdened with a great deal of work and, since they serve usually for very modest fees, they deserve a great deal of credit. They are really the watchdogs of the ordinance and see to it that its spirit and intent are not disregarded. The members of the Board of Appeals are usually appointed by the supervisor or first selectman subject to approval of the rest of the town or village board, and they should be people who have time to devote to such work and have the well-being of the community at heart.

Three Types of Zoning Ordinances

Several types of local ordinances are useful in furthering civic improvement, but the zoning ordinance is probably the one under which most major projects are carried out. Let us re-emphasize at this point that every zoning ordinance, be it for a rural village, a suburban community, a small city, a large metropolis, a county, or a region must be carefully tailored to that particular municipal entity. To borrow an ordinance from another community, however apparently similar, is to court disaster. Unfortunately we cannot deal here with zoning ordinances designed for large cities or metropolitan complexes, nor with county or regional zoning which differ from local municipal zoning principally in that a wider area is covered and hence the regulations may have to be more diversified.

For the remaining communities—small cities, suburban communities, rural villages—the applicable zoning ordinances fall into three general classes. For the small city the ordinance must be intensely concerned with high-density residential land uses, the preservation of existing values, the health and progress of the commercial and industrial part of the community, and with the acquisition and preservation of as much open space, parks, and recreational land as is possible within the city boundaries. Most of these communities have developed to the extent of their legal boundaries and beyond. They cannot control this outer fringe which becomes a problem of the satellite suburban community unless the city can acquire these areas by annexation, or zone them through a cooperative planning agency to which both the city and the suburb subscribe.

A zoning ordinance for a rapidly growing suburban area (and many such areas are without organized local government) or municipality must concern itself with maintaining relatively low-density land uses; encouraging compatible commercial and industrial development to provide local employment and tax revenue; guiding the further growth of the community in desirable directions; preventing undesirable developments; and making prognostications as far into the future as possible to provide for adequate park, open space, and recreational land, and suitable sites for those municipal, commercial, and industrial structures not needed at present but which will, in the foreseeable future, be required to maintain the community as a desirable place to live and work in. It will of necessity be rather detailed and complex.

A zoning ordinance for a more or less static rural or isolated community, on the other hand, should be very simple. It should strive to maintain the existing character of the community (if it is good) or develop a desirable character. It should not be any more restrictive than is absolutely necessary to avoid disaster. It should studiously avoid trying to regulate everything everywhere. It must leave something to the initiative and imagination of the people even though this may occasionally permit something to happen that is less than ideal. It need not be concerned with extremes of population density and land use since it is surrounded by plenty of space. It should, on the other hand, prevent undue crowding, should encourage a high degree of pride in their community on the part of the inhabitants to the end that they will, on their own initiative, maintain their properties in attractive shape and support projects further to beautify their community by developing park lands, open spaces, and recreational areas. It should do something in the direction of avoiding mixed uses in an area but it need not be nearly so adamant about it as would a suburban community or even a city. It should encourage agricultural uses right up to and around the built-up part of the community and have an eye toward forest management and reforestation nearby if this is at all practicable.

Mechanics of Zoning Ordinance

The mechanics of a zoning ordinance have been fairly well standardized. Three principal use districts are usually established as a basis: residential, commercial, and industrial. In a small simple community in all probability no more will be needed. In a more complex one much greater subdivision of use districts is necessary. One basic legal requirement is that all land within the confines of the community be placed in one district or another. In other words it must be comprehensive.

Residential districts may be divided into single-family, two-family, and multi-family dwellings. They may be further divided into districts where the minimum lot size shall be, say, 4000 square feet, the next one 6000 square feet, the next 10,000 square feet, the next half acre, the next one acre, and the least dense two acres. Some communities have gone even further and required, in certain districts for a single-family house site, a minimum of as much as six acres.

Along with these minimum plot sizes go front-, side-, and rear-yard set-back requirements, maximum land coverage, and maximum height of building requirements. This type of ordinance, which has become almost universal, has produced the stratified, regimented, one-class subdivision or suburb which sociologists, and nearly everyone else who has given the matter any thought, deplore.

To overcome this uniformity, in some communities provisions have been made that adjacent, opposite, or diagonally opposite houses must have differing facades. This subject is discussed at greater length under a separate heading (p. 186).

Those who framed the first zoning ordinances were thinking mainly of establishing and maintaining property values, and they thought that by establishing minimum standards these objectives could be accomplished. Others unthinkingly copied their work. It seems fairly evident today that although these ordinances do in fact tend to establish and maintain values in low-density suburbs, they have the opposite effect in those where density is higher. In fact they tend to create future slums because along with small lots go small, cheaply built houses that soon deteriorate. If one small house among other larger ones, or a large one among smaller ones for that matter, deteriorates, as often happens in the older villages, it is a matter of regret but it does not blight the whole neighborhood whereas if the whole street of similar small houses deteriorates the neighborhood character is lost.

Flexible Zoning

It seems to these writers that a different approach to this problem should be made. If, instead of establishing uniform minimum lot sizes, set-backs, and so on for a certain residential district, a minimum population density could be established instead, a builder or developer would be freer in designing his subdivision. He could have some small lots where the terrain is level and larger ones where it is hilly. He would have land left over in most cases that could be acquired by the municipality for park or recreational purposes, and a diversified, interesting, livelier, less-regimented community would result. In the state of New York, under section 281 of the Town Law, the local planning boards have the power to modify the zoning of an area under development in exactly the manner suggested above. To exercise this power wisely and well, the planning board must give the matter more careful study than would be required in processing an ordinary, regimented subdivision map, but it has been done successfully by a few pioneering communities and the idea is well worth further exploration. Additional legislation may be required to make the device work perfectly, but once it is tried its benefits are so obvious that it should not be too difficult to convince the legislature to give the planning boards whatever additional powers they may require to perfect the procedure.

The essential provisions of a zoning ordinance can, therefore, be summarized as follows:

1. Divide entire municipality into use districts: residential, commercial, industrial. These may be further divided if community is complex.
2. List permitted uses. Some ordinances also list prohibited uses, especially obnoxious industries.
3. Establish minimum lot sizes, front-, side-, and rear-yard set-backs. Note should be taken of the fact that minimums tend to become maximums because developers naturally want to get the most out of a tract of land.
4. Establish maximum land-coverage requirements, requirements for access, on-site parking, screen plantings, or other types of barriers.
5. Establish Board of Appeals or Board of Adjustment to:
   a) grant variances in cases of proven hardship or practical difficulties;
   b) interpret ordinance and establish exact district boundaries;
   c) grant permits for special exceptions where designated in ordinance. Adequate standards must be spelled out in the ordinance to guide the board in reaching decisions. Absence of such standards may invalidate decisions.
6. Provide for enforcement. The building inspector is usually the enforcing officer in small communities. In larger ones a special officer may be needed.
7. Append to the ordinance a careful set of subdivision control regulations. These are most important as they contain requirements for street paving, curbs, sidewalks, street trees, drainage structures and catchment basins, and most important of all from the point of view of civic beautification, the establishment of neighborhood parks.

12. Other Applicable Local Laws and Ordinances

Ordinances that can be used to further civic beautification are those governing advertising signs and billboards; the mining of sand, gravel, or other mineral products; and to a limited extent certain others. Some of these may be enacted as part of the zoning ordinance but it is usually considered sounder practice, legally, to keep them separate. This is in case one of these regulatory provisions might be declared invalid by the courts. In such a case, were it a part of the zoning ordinance the whole thing might be thrown out, causing many difficulties and considerable expense to the community, which would have to enact the zoning ordinance over again without the offending clauses.

Sign Ordinances

A sign ordinance, to give it the shorter name, is one that every community can and should adopt. Under the police power, signs overhanging a public way (sidewalk or roadway used by the public whether or not privately owned) can be declared a safety hazard and their removal can be required. Such an ordinance should prohibit the future erection of any such signs and should require the removal of existing ones within a reasonable period, six months to a year depending on circumstances. Signs erected upon or attached to roofs may also be prohibited by law as a safety hazard. The local fire department will be delighted to support such legislation since it realizes the danger such signs can cause if and when a fire occurs in the building on which such signs are located. When it comes to signs attached to the face of a building the problem is not so simple. An ordinance may properly require that they not extend more than a foot or a foot and a half from the face of the building, and a provision in the building code (page 189) may specify how they shall be attached in order to be safe. Ordinances have gone so far as to limit such signs to one for each firm doing business on the premises and to limit their size to a length of 12 or 15 feet, and an area of not more than 150 square feet. Provisions of this sort actually enter upon the field of aesthetic controls and have little to do with health and safety, but we know of no ordinances of this sort that have been declared unconstitutional by the courts.

Size requirements are easy to deal with if the sign is a separate thing built somewhere else and then brought and erected on the building, but if it consists of single letters or other devices attached to the whole face of the building itself, as is frequently done nowadays when the upper stories of older buildings are refaced or modernized, what then is the area of the sign? Is it the whole building face or only the part covered by the letters? This sort of dilemma highlights the difficulty of interpreting and enforcing regulations of this kind. All ordinances should be as clearly written as possible so that there may be no doubt as to what they mean.

Moving signs may be declared to be a traffic hazard and outlawed accordingly. They are, it is claimed, like the Lorelei of old who lured the enchanted seaman to his destruction on the rocks. They often lure the modern motorist to his death by distracting his attention from the business in hand. Illuminated signs may be similarly declared to be a danger and they may also be declared a prohibited use in residential districts because of their incongruity with the residential character of the neighborhood. Free-standing signs may be limited to one for each business establishment. This applies mainly to automobile service stations which use such signs and to those progressive businesses that have set their buildings well back from the highway but that still want to be identified easily by the passing motorist. They should probably not be penalized for having moved back and should be allowed at least one free-standing sign. They need not be enormous, moving, or illuminated. Restraint and good taste obtain in this field as well as anywhere else.

Billboards are a totally different matter. They are defined as advertising signs or devices advertising goods or services NOT obtainable on the premises on which they stand. Under the zoning ordinance they may easily be prohibited in all residential districts as incompatible uses, but in commercial and industrial districts the problem is different since they are, quite truly, a commercial enterprise. The outdoor advertising industry maintains strong lobbies in all states and any attempt to limit billboards, either inside built-up communities or out in the unzoned countryside, is immediately met by strong opposition. It is going to be a long hard fight before they are finally gotten rid of, but that time will come eventually. Meanwhile those individuals and organizations working toward the goal of eliminating billboards from the American scene deserve all the support and encouragement they can get. Actually billboard advertising of nationally sold products has declined in recent years, partly through legislation outlawing them along federally aided highways, but largely because other media like television and mass-circulation magazines offer more for the advertiser's dollar than billboards can. It is possible that this normal attrition plus the diligent work of those who are promoting antibill-board legislation may bring about the desired condition sooner than we had believed possible. This possibility is, however, no excuse to sit back and relax. The battle is not yet won.

Surface Mining Controls

Another prevalent source of ugliness both within and without our communities is surface mining. It may involve either sand or gravel banks, stone quarries, or even strip mining for coal or iron or other minerals. Regulatory measures for controlling such enterprises are within the purview of the zoning ordinance or, lacking such a law, the local communities can adopt special ordinances designed to regulate and control such activities. They may be prohibited entirely in certain districts (usually residential ones), but the main purpose of the law should be to permit within reason logical use of the mineral resources beneath the ground, rather than prohibit what must seem to property owners to be a sensible use of their property. Such ordinances should therefore provide that for safety reasons areas to be excavated shall be fenced and locked at night; that no excavation be undertaken within, say, 25 feet of the boundaries of adjoining property (also for safety reasons to avoid the possibility of earth slippage endangering adjacent lands); that their ugliness be screened by adequate planting within this border strip where no digging will occur; and finally, and most importantly, that after the mining operation is completed the area will be rehabilitated by proper grading. The details of how this work is to be done will have to vary according to the terrain and the location of the property relative to neighboring structures and uses, but the point is that the requirements should be made adequate to restore the mined area to an attractive appearance. There is no reason why, when a mining operation is completed, the area should not be acquired by the municipality for park or recreation purposes, either as a deed of gift as prerequisite to the permit to mine the land, or by purchase for a moderate sum. It is also possible to require the person or corporation mining the land to pay a royalty to the municipality for each ton or cubic yard of material removed. This fee is intended to compensate the community for the cost of issuing the permits and general supervision of the operation and should be scaled accordingly. Since to do so would probaby be held unconstitutional by the courts, such fees cannot be used mainly for revenue.

In some communities threatened by projected mining operations active organizations have come into existence to prevent or regulate them. One such organization called itself CEASE, which letters meant Citizens Effort Against Sandpit Encroachment. It was very effective in enlisting citizen support for suitable legislation.

Street Tree Ordinances

Because street trees are one of the most powerful influences in the direction of civic beauty, as we have seen in Chapter IX, it is almost imperative that a community adopt adequate legislation to protect and care for existing trees and to insure that new ones are planted when old ones are for any reason lost, and to see that in all newly opened subdivisions proper street trees are planted.

In such an ordinance the jurisdiction of the municipality should cover not only the trees along the streets but also those on private property which are within five feet of the front property line, for these, too, serve as street trees. In fact it is often advocated that street trees be planted in such locations for they still shade the street, have a much better chance of survival, and do not interfere with the utility lines or blanket street lighting. Also trees which are on such public property as around public buildings, in squares and parks, or in recreation areas are sometimes included, especially if there is no park department.

The ordinance should also make provision for the hiring of a tree warden who may be either elected or appointed. He should, whenever possible, be an arborist, or at least have considerable knowledge of arboriculture. This is a much more satisfactory plan than the more common practice of putting the enforcement of a street-tree ordinance in the hands of the highway department unless, of course, this department includes a staff person trained for such work.

Some tree ordinances also provide for a public hearing when it is proposed to remove important trees on or near the streets and highways. At such a hearing the whole question of the advisability of the tree removal can be discussed and, if necessary, alternate proposals made. This prevents the sort of thing that happens when a tree—or a whole row of them—is suddenly removed by some authority or other for a street widening or realignment without the ordinary citizens of the area being aware of what is happening until it is too late. By their protests they can often force the authorities to adopt other ways of accomplishing their objective.

Naturally such an ordinance should make proper provision not only for the planting of new trees where needed but also for the care of the existing ones including proper pruning and spraying. Proper feeding should also be included for it does much to improve the health and longevity of trees. There is also often included a provision which requires that any work done by the public utility companies on street trees be approved by and be under the supervision of the tree warden.

Subdivision regulations, which are a part of any well-drawn zoning ordinance, usually require developers to plant trees of an approved variety and size in accordance with definite specifications governing location, spacing, manner of planting, and after care. If this is not so, or if there is no zoning ordinance in effect, then these regulations should be included in the street-tree ordinance.

The great advantage of such an ordinance is that not only are the trees protected and cared for, but these matters become a charge, through taxation, on the whole community which benefits. If enough interest can be aroused in a community so that such an ordinance can be passed, in a short time the community can become famous for its trees.

Parks and Their Maintenance

Every community that has at least one park or recreation area needs a park department as part of the municipal government to maintain these areas. This important and specialized work should not be loaded onto the highway department which is already sufficiently burdened with other matters. Many municipal officials are loathe to see these facilities exist, let alone expand, because they generally mean further expenditure of the municipality's limited funds and man power to care for them. As a result they are often uncared for and instead of being beauty spots enjoyed by all, they present a tired, moth-eaten appearance that is a detriment rather than an asset to the community. Bad park maintenance can give the whole community a run-down, gone-to-seed appearance. Though park maintenance may cost something, it is definitely worth all it costs in community attractiveness. It has been said that a community can afford anything it wants badly enough to vote the necessary money for it.

In any forward-looking community enough enthusiasm can be generated to make certain that a park department is established and staffed with competent people, and that enough money goes into the annual tax levy to permit it to do a decent job. This does not mean extravagance, merely a regard for the proper condition of one's community.

In older communities many small parks will be found to be in need of rehabilitation, restoration, or even redesign. This we have discussed in a previous chapter. Let us mention here only that the burden of initiating and carrying out this work has too often been dropped on the shoulders of a willing but ill-equipped organization like the local garden club. Such organizations rarely are in a financial position to undertake work of this sort, though they are often willing to help in every way they can.

Architectural Controls

Many communities are attempting to further the aims of civic beautification by trying to control the outward appearance of buildings. Many of our older communities, especially the smaller villages in the East, fear that the changes in appearance brought about by the erection of new buildings or the modernization of older ones will destroy the character of the community they so much admire. The cry goes up "let's keep to the Colonial style." Under certain circumstances this is no doubt wise, but the danger lies in a refusal to entertain new ideas or to accept new forms. Incongruity is what is to be avoided whenever possible. Too violent contrasts are often displeasing and a high standard of design in all buildings is something that needs to be encouraged.

To aid in this, architectural boards of review can be established under the zoning ordinance or building code, whose duty it is to pass on all plans for proposed buildings and to suggest modifications that will enhance their attractiveness. This procedure is an adventure into the field of aesthetic control and it is by no means universally approved by the courts. It is therefore wise to proceed in this direction carefully and slowly. Over the years court decisions have tended to broaden the interpretation of the police power to include a certain amount of aesthetic control under the general-welfare clause of the basic law, but progress in this field is by no means uniform. Courts in some jurisdictions have been liberal, others have been adamant in striking down provisions they felt were outside the power of the municipality to enact. When legislation of this sort is tried, one must expect a court fight over it—and possible rejection. However, nothing ventured nothing gained, and if attempts along this line are tried and fail, one should not be too disappointed. At the next attempt they may succeed.

If an architectural review board is established, the greatest care should be exercised in selecting its personnel. They should be people of mature judgment, knowledgeable in the arts and design professions, though not necessarily active practitioners, and should possess unbiased taste. They should be prepared to defend their judgments clearly, but not be discouraged by defeat. In some places, notably Rye, New York, such a board has functioned well for some years and has accomplished much though not, of course, the millennium. It is wise to set one's sights high but be willing to accept less than complete success. Since many decisions of such a board rest on matters of taste, which is a very personal matter indeed, one cannot expect complete agreement with the conclusions reached.

"No Look Alike" Ordinances

Some communities, in an attempt to avoid the sameness that characterizes many contemporary housing developments, have enacted what are known as "no-look-alike" ordinances. These require that houses next to each other, opposite, or sometimes even diagonally opposite, must have differing facades. Not only are such ordinances a severe handicap to a developer, but the acceptable differences in various facades are so small, since the basic plan and mass remain the same, that they are actually ineffective. The result is minor variations but the effect of sameness, or at least too close similarity, remains. The reason these ordinances handicap the developer is that people tend to admire and perhaps buy only one of the three or more models he may erect at the start of the operation. If they do this, he is forced to try to place the same basic house this way or that, use a different facing material on the front, or a false gable here or there to comply with the regulations. This is frustrating, annoys many buyers who may not like the proposed variations from the basic model, and in the end the ordinance accomplishes next to nothing. These writers heartily disapprove such ordinances. Other means for avoiding the regimentation of most housing developments should be found.

Preservation of Historic Sites

In many communities events of historic importance have occurred; famous people have been born, lived, or died; or notable words have been written or spoken. The preservation and maintenance of sites where such events took place may add measurably to the attractiveness of the community. In speaking of the District of Columbia, Justice Douglas of the Supreme Court had this to say, "We do not sit to determine a particular housing project is or is not desirable. The concept of the public welfare is broad and inclusive. The values it represents are spiritual as well as physical, aesthetic as well as monetary. It is within the power of the legislature to determine that the community should be beautiful as well as healthy, spacious as well as clean, well balanced as well as carefully patrolled. If those who govern the District of Columbia decide that the nation's capital should be beautiful as well as sanitary, there is nothing in the Fifth Amendment that stands in the way." This statement, wonderfully broad and inclusive as it is, applies to all that we have been saying in this book so far but particularly, we feel, to the preservation of historic buildings and sites, and that is why we have quoted it at this point.

It has been said with authority that since 1941 from one fourth to one third of the historic and architectural monuments existing at that time have been destroyed by the building of superhighways, housing developments, and other changes wrought, usually, in the name of necessity, expediency or "progress." This wholesale destruction of our cultural heritage from the past must be stopped. The matter is so urgent that an organization known as The National Trust for Historic Preservations has been established with headquarters in Washington, D.C., for the purpose of helping local communities to act affirmatively in this field and to promote interest in a nationwide program of historic preservation.

Although preservation laws are in their infancy, protection of antiquity has been accomplished in the past through the efforts of private individuals or semipublic historical associations, art associations, and other groups. Virginia and New York have witnessed the effective work of such organizations. Over half the states have passed enabling legislation for preservation, maintenance, and regulation of public buildings, parks, landmarks, relics, documents, monuments, and other public property. The Congress has also passed legislation empowering the President to designate such monuments as were deemed historically worthy of preservation, on both federal and private property, to be acquired for the purpose of such preservation. With the exception of New Hampshire (surprisingly) every state has enacted laws designed to support and maintain historic monuments. As is the case with powers delegated by the legislatures to local municipalities to establish planning and zoning, these laws differ from state to state. The first step in a proposed program for the preservation of any historic site must be an examination of the state law under which the project must be carried out, to find out just what is possible and practicable.

From a legal standpoint the preservation of public buildings and sites presents no great difficulty, but the preservation of historic private property is harder to accomplish. The power of eminent domain may, of course, be exercised by the local community to acquire the property for public use by the payment of just compensation, or the police power may be used for the enforcement of regulations for the public good affecting privately owned property available to the public. The first methed is ideal but, carried out to its fullest extent, would be enormously expensive. The second method is cheaper but entails problems of control that are not easy to solve and that often cause friction. Nevertheless it is often the only practicable course to follow. The courts, in a line of important decisions, have attempted to define, limit, and apply the police power in the field of control by states and municipalities of privately owned antiquities and landmarks. Sometimes a group of property owners will band together in an organization to preserve their neighborhood containing things of historic interest from the intrusion of commercialism or other undesirable changes. It should be noted that all sites and monuments privately owned, even if preserved, would not necessarily always be open to the public.

Building Code

Another local code of some importance from the point of view of civic beautification is the building code which is designed primarily to provide that all buildings are structurally safe, but which may incidentally include provisions that tend to improve the appearance of proposed structures (architectural control). This code usually contains rules affecting the manner in which signs may be fabricated and attached to buildings, or the location and structural design of free-standing signs. When writing such provisions the matter of appearance should not be neglected. Building codes may also provide for other features of buildings like overhanging cornices, sun deflectors, marquees, and the like that have an effect on the building's appearance and, consequently, on that of the community, provided these are of a structural nature and not solely designed as ornament.

Fire Code and Others

A fire code, which is also a safety code, may occasionally promote better community appearance by requiring the removal of structures that might be a fire hazard, or roof signs and similar excrescences on buildings. It can also require the removal of accumulations of combustible rubbish from the rear yards of commercial and industrial buildings, and from vacant lots.

Plumbing and sanitary codes, electrical codes, and the housing code do not all have a direct bearing on civic beautification but careful scrutiny of them will often reveal opportunities for the insertion of perfectly legitimate provisions that will also tend to improve community appearance.

In connection with a housing code intended mainly to see to it that housing accommodations are adequate as to space, light and air, and sanitation, something ought to be possible in the way of improvement of the exterior appearance of not only subsidized low-income housing, but middle-income and higher-income housing as well. One can but wonder why most such structures seem always to be drearily ugly. Only the most expensive high-rise apartment buildings in the better parts of our cities have any aesthetic appeal. The rest are purely utilitarian and either dull or downright ugly. Mass housing of one sort or another, as distinguished from single-family private homes either in the city or the suburbs is being constructed at a rapid rate all over the world. In some countries it seems lively, attractive, and provided with many amenities. In the Netherlands, England, the Scandinavian countries, and even Russia this is true. In Greece the buildings are attractive as they rise tier upon tier on the hills around Athens, though the methods of construction used may be open to some criticism. In South America and Mexico many attractive structures have been recently built. In this country we seem to settle for fourteen-story red-brick barracks with or without balconies, but so plain and dull as to appear like traditional prison structures, or rows and rows of two-story so-called garden apartments that provide no gardens, either for individual families or for the group as a whole, but merely open space, grassed or paved, with a few shrubs and trees scattered about without much rhyme or reason. We surely could do much better than this if we were to put our minds on it.

Mobile Homes

Finally, one of the things that bothers most people who take an interest in their community's appearance are the so-called mobile homes or trailers. These have had a rather odd history. Designed originally to be attached to the family touring car for vacation trips, they have evolved, because of the need for housing that could, on occasion, be easily moved from one place to another, into structures that are no longer really mobile but practically permanent fixtures as to location, but still capable of being detached from their site and towed elsewhere. They fill a vast need for housing that is within the means of families of rather limited income who cannot afford to buy a house in a development or suburb and who, because of the vicissitudes of employment, may be required to move about the country from time to time.

There are several good reasons for most communities to resent the intrusion of these mobile homes into their midst. In the first place they are so uncompromisingly ugly that they strike an inharmonious note in any residential community. Hence the tendency is to prohibit them in most residential zones and relegate them to trailer camps. Here they congregate and cause problems of sanitation and other municipal services, to say nothing of the school situation they create. Because they cannot be taxed on the same basis as regular houses, they often do not pay their proportionate share of real-estate taxes, especially school taxes, either directly or through the rent they pay to the owner of the camp. Many communities, therefore, attempt to prohibit their presence within their confines, usually on the basis that their floor area is not sufficient to meet the requirements of the housing code. Since the demand for these structures is very real, this procedure usually results in the establishment of trailer camps just outside the municipal boundaries. This is often no help as the location chosen may well be even more conspicuous than one within the community would have been, and the school-tax problem is often not solved because the school district more often than not extends beyond the municipal boundaries and includes the outside trailer camp.

It would seem that these mobile homes are something we are going to have to live with and that we would be better advised to accept the fact and work toward bettering their appearance than in trying to brush the problem under the rug. Massive pressure ought to be brought to bear on the builders of these things to improve their exterior appearance. Inside they are marvels of well-planned space, but outside they are horrible. This is probably an inheritance from their days as real camping trailers when it was natural and proper to give them a vehicular appearance. Streamlining was then important and other characteristics of design that are appropiate to moving vehicles have been retained. Since movement is no longer the controlling factor, why can they not be made to look like miniature houses? Why do they have to be painted such outrageous colors and be decked out with so much shiny chromium and aluminum trim? It is true that a slight trend toward improvement has appeared and we believe that a thorough rethinking of the design of mobile homes would eliminate many of the objections to them that are now current.

If, instead of trying to get rid of them, the community makes a proper place for them, well chosen for convenience, seclusion from the rest of the community, satisfactory access, drainage, provision of necessary water supply and sanitation facilities, they can be accommodated in the community without their being a blight on the landscape. Provision for adequate space for each unit could be required and the owner of the camp or park site could be required to screen it adequately from adjacent structures or highways by planting or fencing. He could be required to maintain the grounds at a proper standard and provide police control over the area. His rents would probably have to be raised to meet these added costs but in the end a tolerable solution would have been arrived at. Still, one of the main objections to mobile homes and trailer camps has not been solved—the matter of taxation to pay for the necessary community services required. This is a matter that needs further study by the authorities so that a solution which is just to the community and to the occupants of the mobile homes can be arrived at.

13. Urban Renewal and Rehabilitation

Throughout the history of civilization people have drawn together into cities and towns for protection from their enemies and for better and more convenient ways of living. The community provides a much greater opportunity for religious, social, employment, business, and recreational activities than the open country or the very small village can hope to do. In time, however, many if not most of these larger communities suffered obsolescence and decay. For one reason or another they became less desirable residential locations, often owing to massive immigration of poor and poorly educated populations.

Blight and Its Causes

Blight has come about largely because of two things: the population explosion and a widespread flight to the suburbs. These things happened almost simultaneously and provided a gigantic push in the direction of decay for large areas of our major cities and smaller but no less important areas in the smaller cities and towns. The effect of this on the large cities is obvious and catastrophic. But in most towns, or even small rural villages, if you look around you will find smaller or larger pockets of obsolescence and run-down neighbor-hoods. Even rural slums are by no means unknown. Such conditions do not help improve or maintain civic beautification.

Realizing this, community leaders, and through them governmental agencies, began to look for some means of renewing, rehabilitating, and improving these areas of decay and arresting the spread of blight. Everyone knows that such areas breed crime, juvenile and other delinquency, and other undesirable social and economic conditions. Architects, landscape architects, sociologists, and public administrators led the movement to find a solution to the problem. Out of their efforts the Urban Renewal program was born.

Aims of the Urban Renewal Program

Community planning agencies struggling with the present problems of growth and expansion in their communities had little time to devote to large-scale projects for rehabilitation and the rebuilding of run-down areas. Federal and state governments became interested in such projects, however, and as a result a program was established in the Federal Housing and Home Agency (FHHA). Under Title I funds were made available for the necessary planning of the areas to be renewed or rehabilitated and, through the mortgage provisions of the law (Title 701), new construction as well as repair work on older structures was encouraged.

Over 1300 communities of various sizes have taken advantage of this program. Although oriented toward slum clearance in large cities, the program is applicable to smaller communities as well, as is evidenced by the fact that one project, in York, Pennsylvania, consisted of less than half an acre. Larger projects like Eastwick in Philadelphia, however, covered 2500 acres, so the range in size and type of projects is seen to be very wide. Some outstandingly successful projects like Strawberry Bank in Portsmouth, New Hampshire, Philadelphia's Society Hill, New Haven's Wooster Square, and the Custom House in Monterey, California, indicate that great things can be accomplished.

Many projects, however, have been less successful owing, among other things, to poor judgment on the part of those selecting sites to be treated, local politics, bureaucratic red tape, and lack of knowledge and interest in the program on the part of builders who were supposed to come in and buy up the land the project did not need for public purposes, and to build thereon the type of structures the program called for. As time goes on many of these faults will be detected and remedied, but so far the program of urban renewal as a whole has been regarded rather skeptically in many quarters.

Basic Procedures

The procedure is quite complicated. A site has to be selected by the local authorities. If it is approved by the FHHA the community must establish a local agency to operate the project because it is carried out entirely by local people with local funds. The federal government, however, reimburses the local municipality for all planning costs and advances grants or loans for land acquisition. This may range from one sixth to three fourths of the total cost depending on the circumstances. The community, in lieu of cash, may furnish such things as new streets, utilities, and the like.

The planning of the project, which is done locally though paid for by the federal government, is the most important phase of the whole endeavor. This planning is best done by a professional planner, landscape architect, or an architect, or better yet by all three professions working together as a design and planning team with, of course, competent engineering assistance.

If a suitable site is selected the community, through urban renewal, not only rids itself of a deteriorating neighborhood, but also stands to gain school sites, parks, playgrounds, and other community amenities. It can require that the area be rebuilt in whatever manner it decides is most suitable. This is where the civic beautification approach is possible. There is no reason at all why an urban-renewal area, when completed, should not add immensely to the good appearance of the entire community. Not only will it be attractive in itself but its presence will often stimulate surrounding areas in their efforts to improve and rehabilitate themselves and to arrest the creeping progress of blight.

The objects of urban-renewal and rehabilitation programs can be briefly summarized as (1) to get rid of obsolescent, decayed areas in our towns and cities; (2) to provide an opportunity to substitute superior construction and design for poor design and shoddy construction; (3) to provide an opportunity (because funds are available) to preserve and restore important historic buildings and sites; (4) to widen the field of opportunity for civic beautification and embellishment; (5) to provide sites for needed municipal structures, recreation areas, and the like.

These programs are not primarily slum clearance, though they may and often do result in removing slum buildings, and of course their inhabitants, from an area. They may involve clearing the area completely, known as the bulldozer approach, or in selective removal of worn-out buildings with retention and remodeling of the better ones.

At first most of the programs stressed the complete clearance of the site. In following this procedure many good buildings, and some, though not of important historic interest but of sufficient age and character to give a desirable atmosphere to the area or the community as a whole, were destroyed. This approach was finally recognized as misdirected and the emphasis today is more on rehabilitation and reconstruction than on total demolition.

As these programs were first set up the municipality, after

having planned the area, took title to all the land, cleared the site, selected those parts of it that should be retained for schools, parks, or other municipal purposes, and then sold the remaining land to private developers who would then construct apartment houses, commercial buildings, or whatever else the planners proposed for the area. Unfortunately the old proverb about the horse and the drink of water came into play. Frequently private developers either wanted to build something entirely different from what the planners had proposed or were not interested in doing anything at all in this particular area. Therefore the difficulty of disposing of the surplus land developed and many projects were stymied at this point. All projects were supposed to be ultimately self-liquidating, but few have reached this desirable goal.

It appears, therefore, that before a community enthusiastically plunges into an urban-renewal program it should be very certain that the area to be renewed is a practical one on which to begin operations under these programs. It should also be very certain that the planning consultants it engages are fully competent, not only to provide superior design services, but to master the intricacies of governmental procedures. This is a combination of talents not to be found around every corner.

Site Selection

The selection of an area to become an urban-renewal project is often very difficult. Not all run-down, decrepit areas are suitable since one of the essential characteristics of the area is that it can presumably be developed in such a way that the investment will be self-liquidating. In other words, monies advanced by the federal and state governments for planning, land purchase, and site clearing should return in the form of sale price of surplus land. This is an ideal condition seldom realized. Usually the cost of the site improvements are paid for by the municipality and, of course, the cost of any buildings to be used by the municipality for any purpose, or the development of parks and playgrounds, would not normally be recouped. In any case the possibility of profitable sale of land not needed for these purposes must be considered in selecting a project site.

Blight does not stand still and when its beginnings can be detected in time and suitable steps taken to reverse the downward trend, its spread can be halted. Rather than select a site for renewal that is really gone too far, it is often wiser to select one where blight has begun and the area is not too far gone. These areas have the strength and vitality to enable them to respond to the stimulus of preventive and rehabilitation procedures. It is easier to protect what is good and fix it up than to go to the expense of clearing the whole site and starting anew.

At the beginning eliminate from consideration those areas unquestionably good enough as they are. These need not be high-class, high-income areas. All they need be is decent, respectable, well-maintained housing or commercial properties. Total clearance areas, on the other hand, will be those that can only be benefited by a process of total demolition and reconstruction. In between are many areas that need sometimes more, sometimes less, rehabilitation, redesign, and reconstruction. To narrow the field of selection still further those areas that need some renewal but which have sufficient strength so that they can do their own face-lifting job with, one hopes, some advisory help from the municipal authorities, can be eliminated. What such areas often lack is motivation and this can often be supplied by local groups interested in civic beautification and improvement. This leaves those areas in a community, be they large or small, residential, mixed, commercial or industrial, that require more help than they can themselves supply, as fit subjects for an urban-renewal project.

Relocation Problems

Danger exists that our thinking about proposed projects will center around some particular phase to the exclusion of other important factors. It may be that the area under consideration contains many run-down dwellings, either single- or multi-family, where an unfortunate group of people live who, for one reason or another have drifted into the neighborhood. If we think only of their wretched hovels and forget that they constitute a homogeneous social or racial enclave, and that they would find it difficult, if not impossible, to reorient their lives to either dispersal into other neighborhoods or rehousing on the same site in new, unfamiliar buildings, we may miss one of the essential characteristics of good urban renewal which is, brutally stated, not to disrupt the social structure of the community but to reinforce and strengthen it.

All too many renewal projects have required that the residents of the site be forceably removed to other locations much against their will. Also many areas have been rebuilt in such a manner that even though families move back to the same location they formerly occupied, conditions have been so radically changed that they find their new homes uncongenial. This was the main reason why the early "cities beautiful" of England were not unqualified successes, and why the more recent "satellite towns" near London have had to make major changes.

One thinks of the Greek island of Santorini. Through devastation by a severe earthquake most of the homes of the inhabitants were destroyed. In the interest of safety the government built new homes far back from the cliff edge. But the people, accustomed to living on the brink of a precipice, would have none of them. They rebuilt their homes right where they had formerly been, danger from earthquake or no.

What has happened to many small businesses forced to relocate on account of some urban-renewal project is nothing short of tragic. These businesses depend on local custom and, if this is removed or they themselves are forced to go elsewhere, they seldom survive. So far little consideration has been given to their plight. A well-trained and benevolent sociologist in the urban-renewal administration would probably see to it that this sort of thing could not happen. He would think of these problems whereas the architect or engineer would be likely to overlook them.

Identity of Neighborhood

An area selected for urban renewal should have an identity of its own. It should be clearly separated from other areas by such easily recognized boundaries as major highways, topography, or land use. It should be oriented to some focal point, like all good design, such as a church, school, park, or shopping district around which the life of the area revolves. If it is a central commercial area this focal point could well be the largest department store in town, the hotel, even a theater or auditorium and, certainly the municipal building complex—town hall, fire station, and so on. The area should have common characteristics and common problems, both social and physical. Thus so prosaic a thing as a railroad station could serve as a focal point, though to be effective it should be much more attractive than such structures usually are, and some other facilities should be grouped with it. If it is primarily a residential area its focal point can be the local elementary school, a church or a group of churches around a small park, or even a well-designed and properly located neighborhood shopping center.

The character of a neighborhood is something one feels rather than consciously sees. It is made up of such factors as pleasant openness or well-organized closeness, variety of building placement and types, good architectural design, and good plantings. A neighborhood that possesses a good character is likely to mellow and improve with age given, of course, decent maintenance and sufficient interest in their surroundings on the part of the inhabitants. When an area to be selected for renewal has this kind of character and charm every effort should be made to preserve and enhance it. This quality has been the essential ingredient in many cases where an old area has succeeded in maintaining its vitality and staged a successful comeback even after blight had seriously set in. Georgetown in the District of Columbia is an outstanding example, and Jane Jacobs in her book *The Death and Life of Great American Cities* cites the north end of Boston as another.

Rehabilitation of Fine Old Areas

But regardless of how much charm and character an area may have it cannot be a fit subject for urban renewal unless it can be made adaptable to present-day needs and preferences. This applies both to building types and the surrounding area. In almost every community, groups or whole streets of fine old houses of monstrous proportions can be found slowly falling into decay because the original owners are long since dead and gone and few families nowadays can afford to maintain them or would if they could. These buildings often have great architectural merit or, if not, they at least express the taste of their era and should remain as living examples of the past. Notable streets of this sort are East Avenue in Rochester, New York, and Euclid Avenue in Cleveland, the main street of Cortland, New York, and many, many others.

The beginnings of a movement by large families to forsake their cramped contemporary homes and return to living in these larger, older houses can be detected here and there. It is to be hoped that this trend continues and expands to considerable proportions. Older structures are not only usually more commodious than newer ones but they offer fascinating opportunities for restoration, reconstruction, or modernization. Since in most communities these older places are given an obsolescence credit with respect to their assessment for tax purposes, their position taxwise tends to be favorable.

Some of these houses can be converted into multi-family buildings without destroying their architectural character. Others can be converted into institutional or commercial uses of many sorts. Others present insurmountable problems, not the least of which are the arbitrary and restrictive zoning ordinances and building codes in force in many communities. These ordinances are intended to insure health, safety, and general welfare but they are often used to force the destruction of many fine buildings which cannot practically be made to conform to them. Often these provisions are purely arbitrary and not at all realistic, but they are frequently supported vociferously by residents of the neighborhood and surrounding areas who wish to maintain their neighborhoods as they are, and fear that by allowing practical changes in these older houses they may be endangering their own property values. This is often not true, but the problem is frequently misunderstood and, as a consequence, ill-advised action is taken and often blight begins to creep into the neighborhood.

The area chosen for renewal should also be one that offers a good possibility of long-term stability. If it does not appear to possess this characteristic an effort to conserve it may be hazardous. An area of high turnover, either by residents or businesses moving in and out, or one that appears likely to be soon overrun by incompatible uses, such as industry moving into a residential or commercial area, or business or institutional uses moving in among residences, indicates a lack of stability. Also if the area is threatened by a new superhighway or is about to be flooded for a reservoir, or become a part of a restricted watershed area, it is unsuitable for renewal or rehabilitation on a long-term basis.

In some areas street systems and public utilities can practically be rearranged and adapted to redevelopment. In others this is so costly a procedure that renewal is impracticable. Close proximity to desirable areas is an advantage as these desirable areas exert a pull in the right direction. In selecting an urban-renewal area it is important to distinguish between the problems that can and those that cannot be solved through rehabilitation. If the buildings are too far gone or too poorly constructed in the first place; if provisions for necessary utilities would prove so costly as to be out of proportion to the revenues the property could be expected to yield; if after the project is completed no one wants to live there anyway, the area should not become the subject of a renewal project. When adverse uses dominate the area it is questionable whether renewal is possible. If they do not dominate, then rehabilitation is possible and desirable. It must be remembered that in any rehabilitation project as distinguished from complete renewal the owners of the various properties must pay for improvements to their own buildings and their willingness to do so will be based largely on whether or not they believe that by so doing they will provide better living conditions for themselves and their families in a home they own.

Major vs. Minor Projects

Very often quite minor improvements and changes in an area can transform it from a potentially depressed area into one that is on the way up. If harmful, incompatible land uses, like an abandoned factory among residences, can be eliminated; if poor circulation can be improved by minor street realignment, extensions, closings and the like, and if heavy traffic can be diverted from the area; and if adequate attention is given to the matter of street trees and suitable plantings in those areas where such a thing is possible, dull, dead, downward-moving areas will perk up remarkably quickly to the satisfaction of everybody.

What was accomplished in Philadelphia by Mrs. James Bush-Brown and the Neighborhood Garden Association should be more widely known, for it is an indication of what is possible given the right sort of leadership. Several blocks in one of the worst slum areas of the city were cleaned up and beautified by installing window boxes and small door-yard gardens. By the third year of the project over 3000 window boxes had been installed in 63 blocks, vacant lots had been cleaned up, fences whitewashed, and many improvements made within the houses by the tenants themselves. The project was well organized and a highly successful example of inexpensive but effective urban renewal and civic beautification done without the aid of any governmental agency. Many other similar instances could be cited throughout the country. These are steps in the right direction.

Successful examples of urban-renewal projects are somewhat difficult to find. One of the earlier ones, and one applicable to even the smallest community, is Stony Brook, Long Island, New York. Mr. Ward Melville became interested in this little community back in 1949. He bought up the existing commercial buildings, which were few and undistinguished but old, and rebuilt the place with the assistance of a competent architect. The style chosen was early American and the result is charming though perhaps in a nostalgic sort of way.

The project still exists in its original form with few additions. It is well kept up and, according to Mr. Melville, pays a reasonable annual profit. As he says, it could have been done by the local residents and merchants themselves, but they lacked leadership which, with the necessary financing, Mr. Melville provided. Obviously this project was neither slum clearance nor civic beautification as such but it provided both.

For two widely different examples, look at Rockefeller Center in New York City, which certainly was urban renewal as the site was completely cleared before being rebuilt, and which has been immensely profitable; and Colonial Williamsburg, more a restoration than a renewal, which is also a successful and profitable venture. These examples are hardly applicable to the average small town or city but they do illustrate that one of the basic needs of a successful urban-renewal program is superior leadership and superior design. All these examples had it, but many others have not and that is one of the reasons why they failed.

14. Professional Help for Civic Beautification

All civic-beautification projects will benefit if professional advice is sought and applied to them. This is particularly true of large-scale projects, but the smaller ones are also likely to turn out much better if they have had some professional help. This need not be much more than a review of the plans and specifications by a professional to guard against impractical ideas or inefficient procedures. The writers have reviewed many plans for such things as simple plantings around a monument or honor roll, at the entrance to a community, along a particularly uninteresting roadside that needs a touch of beauty, and other projects of a similar nature.

A great deal of credit must be given to garden clubs who have initiated many such projects. They deserve all the help they can get to further their aim of making and keeping America beautiful. Because they stir up interest and excitement over the conditions existing in a community and lead to improvement, these modest attempts at civic beautification are most important. It is deplorable, however, that much of this work is fragmentary, trivial, temporary, and poorly designed and executed. Professional help on them would avoid many of these shortcomings.

Substantial civic-beautification programs cannot be accomplished in an uncoordinated, impulsive, short-sighted manner. For any effort to make a real contribution it must be part of a community-wide program and it must have professional guidance. We feel that it is the duty of professionals practicing in a community to proffer such help as a civic duty, not necessarily without charge, of course, but at least at a price the sponsoring organization can afford.

The question of who shall provide this guidance immediately arises. Some will look toward the engineering profession. Others will think of architects or town planners as the right persons to go to. Often nonprofessional people like nurserymen, landscape contractors, and gardeners will be called upon. But the one professional who is fully qualified in this field is the landscape architect. All the others approach it from a limited point of view.

The engineer thinks in terms of mathematics which he translates into specifications for grading, road alignment and construction, paving, drainage, and the like. His skills are necessary, but since his training is generally not oriented in the direction of aesthetics, his contribution should be confined to those phases of the problem that lie within his field of competence. He should not be expected to make decisions involving aesthetic considerations.

Architects are, of course, trained to think largely but their main interest is the individual building as an entity, less so as a part of the landscape. They are becoming increasingly concerned, however, with urban design and are making substantial contributions in this field, especially in the redesign of the core areas of the larger cities and towns. Architects are vitally interested in aesthetics and they can contribute a great deal in discussions dealing with problems of civic beautification.

Professional planners, who belong to a fairly recently recognized profession which has stemmed from both architecture and landscape architecture, are taught to think in terms of people, how they live, how they get from place to place, how they spend their free time, and similar things. They are, therefore, usually more concerned with the planning problems that embrace the entire city, town, county, or even region. Although it is true that their training includes a great deal of what is ordinarily considered either architecture or landscape architecture, they are generally more concerned with the practical aspects of living and business conditions of the community than with its beautification.

Only landscape architecture combines in its disciplines all these skills. The landscape architect's interests are the broadest, embracing not only the practical side of laying out land for use but also the social and aesthetic aspects of civic beautification. This thesis may seem revolutionary to many, and certainly contrary to current practice. Can it be justified?

Usually when a project to build something is started, an architect is first engaged, then a builder and finally, if at all, a landscape architect to plant a few bushes and trees around it. Unfortunately this often results in the building being poorly sited, incorrectly oriented, and poorly related to neighboring structures. The floor elevations may be incorrectly established resulting in either a drainage or terracing problem and great difficulty in properly integrating the landscape development with the living portion of the building. Often, too, approaches such as driveways and walks may have been thoughtlessly located.

When a project to lay out a street, subdivision, or even a park or playground is discussed, an engineer is brought in to see that the area is properly graded, drained, and paved. Only then is the landscape architect brought in for the purpose of "decorating" it with suitable planting. By that time it is often discovered that it is too late to save valuable trees and other natural features of the site, that the area has been so cut up with permanent improvements that it is impossible properly to locate the various features the project is supposed to provide, be they homes, playfields, or areas of quiet natural beauty.

When a project for urban renewal is proposed, a professional planner is the one people turn to in search of a solution to the problem. After the bulldozers have done their work and the area is ready for reconstruction, the landscape architect may be called in to suggest street trees and screen plantations. Very probably no thought has been given to the aesthetic aspects of the project. It may turn out to be as banal and ugly as the structures it has displaced. No provisions for parklets where people can rest and relax, no provisions for adequate shade and greenery have been made. In other words nobody has given any thought to the aesthetic aspects of the project.

All too often the "dressing up" of a building or an urban-renewal project, or one designed for civic beautification is turned over to some local landscape contractor, nurseryman, or gardener for planting. These specialists are chiefly concerned with plants or the construction of walks, driveways, walls, and lawns. They are usually untrained in design and are, of course, strictly commercial rather than professional in their approach. They have much to contribute but they should work only under the guidance of a landscape architect. Generally they prefer to do this rather than to be put in a position of responsibility in matters of design and aesthetics.

That people generally think of the landscape architect as someone who comes in at the tail end of a project is largely the fault of the profession itself which has not presented to the public a true and proper image. It has permitted the public to think of it as a group of dilettantes whose principal interest is either in large private estates or in incidental planting to embellish the work of other professions. This is a tragic mistake that will probably take a long time to correct. Meanwhile the particular skills the profession is prepared to contribute to our contemporary civilization are largely being wasted.

From the beginning through the centuries, in war or peace, civilized order or barbarism, the creation and design of human environment was in the hands of rulers, conquerors, and their henchmen, or colonial impresarios and land speculators. Perhaps, strangely, no one thought of it as a possible professional activity. Barbers became surgeons; those who could read and write in an otherwise illiterate civilization became lawyers; builders became architects or engineers; herbalists became doctors, but nobody thought that the business of laying out land for human purposes deserved professional status. When any such activity was required, the architects, the engineers, or the horticulturalists took care of it.

Many eminent people worked in this field. During the Renaissance Palladio, Vignola, and Leonardo da Vinci. Le Nôtre who lived somewhat later thought and worked in Renaissance terms. In England Kent, Brown, and Repton accomplished much. In the 19th and early 20th centuries Lutyens carried on in similar vein. In this country William Penn, Lord Oglethorpe, and Thomas Jefferson contributed their abilities and we borrowed L'Enfant from France to lay out the city of Washington. In the 19th century Frederick Law Olmsted, Sr., Calvert Vaux, his partner, and Charles Eliot followed in the footsteps of Andrew Jackson Downing. But none of these people, with the exception of Olmsted and Eliot, called himself a landscape architect or thought of himself as such. Around the turn of the century, however, the term landscape architect began to come into use, and the profession of landscape architecture took its place among the design professions.

Immediately professional status was established, specialization developed. Some landscape architects, like Manning and Nolen, devoted most of their time to city planning. They laid great stress on planned improvements versus haphazard growth. They realized the importance of open space in cities and the necessity of acquiring land well ahead of need so that it could be had at a cost within the means of the community. Others in the profession like the Olmsted office, Charles W. Leavitt, Charles Downing Lay, O. C. Simonds, and others divided their time between private-estate work and the field of city planning and urban design. More recently some landscape architects have devoted their energies to regional considerations on a vast scale including national and state parks. This specialization continues to exist today. Those who work mainly on urban renewal and slum-clearance problems find themselves working closely with architects and sociologists. Because their work, of necessity, emphasizes the use of trees and shrubs those who work in the private property field find that they are often mistakenly regarded as interested almost exclusively in planting. In fact the word "landscaping" has come into use meaning the embellishment of a property with plant material. It is, to all practical purposes, synonymous with the word "gardening." A landscape architect is not a "landscaper" in this sense. His field of competence is much wider than the word implies. He, and all members of his profession, are mainly concerned with the broad development of any piece of property for use and beauty with or without incidental planting.

Any space—whether it be a parking lot, a private estate of whatever size, a town, city, or regional area, the surroundings of a public, commercial, or industrial building or building complex, a college or university campus or other school grounds—presents problems within the field of competence of landscape architecture. The range is almost infinite. It extends into the fields of architecture, engineering, and planning and to draw lines definitely separating these professions is, for practical purposes, impossible. Nor is there any need to. If he is trained and competent an architect may, quite properly, lay out the grounds around his building. If he has a feeling for it an engineer can design the lines and grades for a highway. A planner may indicate where in the community he would encourage various land uses, including parks and playgrounds, and how they might be brought into being.

Though planning is nowadays recognized as a separate profession it is, in essence, a synthesis of the skills of the landscape architect, the architect, the engineer (all members of the design professions), and such others as sociologists, lawyers, public administrators, traffic experts, housing specialists, and many others. The field is large and any one individual is unlikely to possess all the necessary skills to carry through a successful project. On any project of considerable extent teamwork is therefore desirable. The ideal situation comes into being when the landscape architect, the architect, the engineer, and the planner are brought together at the very inception of the project so that each can contribute his skills and technical knowledge at the appropriate time and place.

This team approach is an ideal setup for any civic beautification project of any size. If the team is not to get bogged down in quarrels and obstructive tactics by one or another of the group, it needs a strong personality to head it. Professional jealousy does exist and it must be recognized as one of the facts to be considered in setting up a project of this sort. Where the community has established an urban-renewal program, it is possible that the urban-renewal director could serve as head of the team since he is presupposed to be an expert administrator and usually not a member of any of the design professions. He can, therefore, more easily adopt an impartial attitude. Such a person should never be selected for political reasons, though he sometimes is.

Under the guidance of a competent administrator, a professional person, or a team of such experts, a civic group—be it a garden club, service club, youth group, church-affiliated organization, or whatever—may proceed with a civic beautification project knowing that its efforts will be well directed, that inefficiency and waste will be reduced or happily eliminated entirely, and that the final result will be a real benefit and permanent asset to the community.

Good, enduring design is the objective, not transitory "beautification" that is merely temporary surface decoration. Only under professional guidance can this sort of design be produced. This fact need not discourage those who want to do something about the appearance of the community. The field is large and there is room for many sorts of projects. There are those that a small interested group can properly handle, and there are those that require a larger, more expert organization. To differentiate clearly between the two sorts, and to avoid spending effort on something either too big for one's resources, or too small to be worth while, is half the battle. The fight against ugliness will, perhaps, never be fully won, but any improvement in the appearance of our surroundings will be for the better, and surely with the necessary will on the part of everyone concerned, much progress is possible.

15. Organization for a Project

Those readers who have stayed with us to this point are probably ready to ask the all-important question, "How do we begin?" At least we hope we have aroused enough enthusiasm to cause such a question to be asked and an answer demanded. Along the way we have dropped a few hints such as getting to know how your planning board works; getting in touch with your local officials, park department, highway department and such; looking up the laws that may affect what you propose to do; enlisting professional advice from local architects and landscape architects and other influential citizens; inquiring about financing, and all the other important things. But we probably have not been as specific as one might wish. Unfortunately it is impossible to be as definite about how to go about accomplishing a civic beautification or improvement project as one would like to be, simply because conditions surrounding such endeavors vary so greatly from place to place, time to time, and according to who is engaged in them. There are, however, certain steps that have to be taken in connection with any project which we will try to set forth.

Any civic project, like all Gaul, is divided into three parts. There is the part having to do with the inspiration for the project, its planning, financing, and the business of organizing how it is to be done and by whom. Then comes the second part, the actual carrying out of the project itself. Finally the third part which is to foster continuing interest in it, seeing to it that it is properly maintained, and if possible expanded into other similar projects in the future.

Origin of a Project

Projects usually originate as ideas in the mind of some one individual. He gets a bee in his bonnet, so to speak, and begins to talk about it to his friends, at meetings of organizations to which he belongs, to local officials, and to anybody who is willing to listen. From these casual conversations a nucleus of an organization begins to emerge to be later expanded into a full-scale project.

Both the practical and aesthetic success of every civic-development project depends on how well it is organized. Time spent on this phase of the enterprise is always well spent, although if it takes more than a minimum amount of time it may appear to be holding back progress. Without a sound organization, however, any project is all too likely to degenerate into a mass of loose ends, personal disagreements, lack of drive, and final failure.

During the first phase of the project the work of a single person or a very small group, promoting the idea here and there on all and sundry occasions, is mainly what is needed. Intense enthusiasm must be generated by this small group in the minds of a great many people before the project is announced publicly, formal organization brought into being, and final commitment to the project made. This small group or steering committee should be so carefully chosen that the continuation of an adopted policy and sustained interest in it is assured. Large unwieldy committees, especially during the first phases of the project, are to be studiously avoided. They almost always slow down progress of the work and, by bringing in too many differing points of view at this stage, tend to weaken it. Later on large advisory committees are necessary, provided their tendency to take it over, or to "advise" to a point where they so change the project as to damage it, is controlled. Their main purpose is to broaden the base of support within the community and spread it out to include other groups than the one that originated the idea. They are often useful to solicit necessary financing, to press for required legislation, and to combat the opposition of lobbies and other special interests. The hard-core committee, as one might call it, should, however, never lose control of the project it has initiated to other persons or groups.

Pilot Projects

Project selection, as we have indicated, is of utmost importance. We have stressed the need to make a thorough survey of the community before deciding on what to try to accomplish. This need for a study of the community in depth need not, however, prevent the undertaking of obviously necessary projects at once, while enthusiasm for them is at a high peak. Survey or no survey, in every community there will be obvious places where something to improve or beautify the town, village, city, or neighborhood should be started right away, sometimes to protect something of value that is threatened with destruction, sometimes to remove an eyesore, sometimes to create something beautiful for its own sake. The only things to be sure of in connection with such a pilot project are (1) that financial support for it is available and (2) that it is not in the way of some project the local government has determined upon but may not yet have announced publicly.

Community Survey

In making a community survey it is wise to adopt a standard form of questionnaire, as it were, so that not only all points of importance will be covered by those making the survey, but also so that the information obtained will be comparable. Margherita Tarr, Extension Landscape Architect at Iowa State University, has designed such a form which she has used with success in her work. We are including at the end of this chapter a somewhat abbreviated version of this form which will be of help to any community making a similar survey. As will be noted, this form lists such aspects of the area as its topography, natural features, and man-made historical features. It asks questions having to do with the impression one gains when taking a look at a town and its environs. Answers to these questions will indicate pretty completely what the community needs as well as what it has, and how it goes about its business of daily living.

Small Projects

A word of warning must be given again and again. Avoid the small trivial projects, the ones that are mere prettification, the ones that lack financial backing or the assurance of good maintenance! Untold hours of hard work have been wasted on this sort of endeavor, with a net result so insignificant as to be negligible. Small projects should not be condemned as such, since they may lead to greater interest in civic beautification on the part of more people and may be expanded later on into programs of greater size and significance. If they are part of a well-thought-out plan for civic beautification they are worth while, but if they are merely isolated, inconspicuous, and without significance for the community as a whole they are best avoided.

To show how small projects may be developed into a full-scale program, consider the case of the garden club that decided to do a small planting around a public building. The project was successful and called attention to the fact that the community as a whole needed a thorough face lifting, especially around the civic center. The aura of success is contagious. Once people see a beauty spot that has been created by their friends and neighbors, they become interested in developing and improving their own neighborhoods, the town or city, or the surrounding region. Professionals become involved, the local government gets into the act, and the first thing one knows a full-scale rehabilitation of the community is in full swing.

In selecting projects an eye to popular appeal is important. If a community swimming pool is needed, for instance, the service clubs—Lions, Rotary, Kiwanis, Elks, or other fraternal organizations—are certain to be interested in it and give their full support. The project can often, later on, be expanded to a community-wide recreational program and even to the acquisition of open land outside the community for future recreational use, or for its own sake.

The community-wide survey, the need for which we must continue to stress, will emphasize different aspects of the community, depending on who makes it. Everyone engaged in making it will have his or her pet projects or predilections and it is therefore wise to have as many differing sorts of people and opinions represented as possible. Garden-club members, for instance, will be particularly interested in street trees and other planting projects. Roadside committees will have roadside improvement, removal of signs, and cleanup in mind, including suitable planting projects. Social and charitable agencies will stress better housing and youth activities, including recreation of all sorts, as their objective. The service clubs will probably concentrate their attention on recreation both of the organized variety and camping, hiking, fishing, and hunting in the wild areas around the community, if any such remain available. P.T.A. mothers, too, will be interested in recreational facilities and in the control of traffic, especially near schools. Businessmen will clamor for more parking and a solution to the general traffic problem, and real-estate people and developers will be interested in any proposed legislation that may affect their operations.

When this massive survey has been completed it must be carefully evaluated and some sort of time schedule developed listing the various projects that have come to light in the order of their importance, size, and feasibility. It may appear that a pilot project should be initiated at once to test community responsiveness, and this must be carefully selected with that fact in mind. Financing, government cooperation, and all such basic factors must be explored and a policy in regard to them formulated.

Really large projects, like urban renewal, because they require the approval and cooperation of government agencies at different levels, may require that a large committee, or a group of committees, be formed to carry the word back to the various organizations the members represent, but the small originating committee should by some means maintain as much control over it as possible. It can often do this by having its members serve as chairmen of the various subcommittees.

On any project of considerable size definite plans and specifications prepared by qualified professionals must be commissioned, accepted, and paid for before the work starts. Financial assistance for professional help in planning is sometimes available from various funds and agencies. Only with professional help at this stage can the sponsoring committee assure itself that the work will be done efficiently and economically, and that essential aesthetic considerations have not been overlooked. These professionally prepared plans and specifications lift the project out of the amateur class. Well-prepared plans are one of the best means of securing publicity for the project and for enlisting the support of various groups and individuals in the community who need to be shown what is proposed in graphic form. When people can see where their money is to be spent, they are much more likely to be liberal in donating it or voting for the use of tax funds than they are if the project remains nebulous. Therefore, the money expended for professional assistance is never wasted.

Publicity

In arranging for publicity, remember that names are always newsworthy. Get well-known people to serve on the general committee, let their names appear on the project committee's letterhead, cut ribbons on opening day and the like, but don't let them tell the steering committee how to run the show. Never put someone on the steering committee merely for his name. Never tell anyone that he or she will not have to do anything. Dead wood on a committee is as useless as dead wood anywhere else. Professional people are particularly valuable committee members. Architects, landscape architects, lawyers, engineers, builders, all have more than nominal interest in community affairs and whatever may affect its life. Their cooperation should always be enlisted.

To facilitate almost any project for civic improvement and beautification the public must be educated to realize the necessity, the soundness, and the value of the project. Only by publicity can opposition born of ignorance or misinformation be forestalled. And only through the widespread dissemination of information about the project can support for either fund raising through voluntary subscription or for allocation from municipal sources be obtained.

Thus it becomes evident that one of the most important of the various committees will be the one which deals with education and publicity. As a part of this educational process all the various media of advertising (except billboards and signs) and news dissemination should be utilized to the fullest extent. A speaker's bureau should also be organized to provide competent speakers who are willing to give their time to attend meetings of various organizations to explain what is proposed and to ask for help and cooperation. All such talks and the material used in press releases, advertisements, or on TV and radio must not only be factually correct down to the smallest detail but they should be so presented as to have news value.

Finance and Ways and Means

Among the most important subcommittees will be those dedicated to finance and ways and means. The first develops estimates of the cost of the project and the second goes about the business of finding the money.

The finance committee should have among its members an expert on finance, such as a prominent banker, and a professional person (architect, landscape architect, or engineer) who knows about construction costs. Some member of this committee, probably the banker, should be designated as the treasurer.

The ways and means committee needs among its members diligent workers who are willing to devote plenty of time to the work and who know how to approach all sorts of persons and organizations in search of financial support.

Approaching the elected officials of a community is one of the most difficult but necessary steps that must be taken before a project is launched not only for their cooperation but also to ask for financial support. They are always critical of any proposal to spend public funds which they usually guard as though they were their own. On the other hand they are constantly trying to maintain before the public an acceptable image so that they may comfortably continue in their present positions or move up to more important ones at future elections. This being the case, if a project appeals to them as a potential asset to their careers, they will support it. To qualify for official support a project must, therefore, be well planned, financially sound, must contribute to the health, safety, and welfare of the community, and must be politically expedient. By the way, if public credit for their support can be graciously conceded to public officials, even making the idea of the whole thing appear to be their brain child, so much the better.

When the project is large enough and benefits a wide area, funds from county, state, and even the federal government may, under certain circumstances, be made available. In some states the Department of Commerce or the Department of Industrial Development can make funds available for planning studies that will lead to the adoption of permanent planning programs and zoning controls. They may be willing to supply expertly trained personnel to help the local community in its efforts. Financial assistance for planning under certain circumstances is available through FHHA.

Cooperation of Private Organizations

Some of the great private foundations can be induced to make grants-in-aid, particularly for projects that will help relieve bad social conditions, combat delinquency, or promote health. Such grants are usually made on very liberal terms that permit the community to extend the time of repayment considerably.

Another agency of great importance is the Nature Conservancy that is devoted to the acquisition of land to protect and preserve open space and natural beauty spots. A certain large mercantile corporation provides funds to local groups as an incentive to civic beautification. This program is run mainly through the Federated Garden Clubs and consists of a series of local competitions for designs and projects indicating civic responsibility and improvement. The program is immensely successful, not only in arousing local interest in civic projects, but in improving their quality through keen competition on the local level. It should, however, consider more carefully than it does the need for professional help and guidance in these projects which have a regrettable tendency to be amateurish and somewhat trivial. Some of the various state Roadside Committees also sponsor contests, and the General Federation of Women's Clubs has a Community Achievement contest.

Though the idea that one should make no little plans is valid, neither should a committee become involved with some grandiose scheme that it will be unable to finance or properly carry out. Careful evaluation from all angles before final commitment to the idea is essential. If a project is a really big one, too much to attempt right at the start, it is usually possible to begin on one phase of it in a small way and then, when that has been successfully completed, move on to larger things. A successful accomplishment, even though small, is a big help in eliciting support for further endeavors. A cleanup campaign, for instance, that might be an initial starter, will bring forceably to the attention of everyone how badly the community needs a more intensive program of rebuilding, reconstruction, and general improvement.

Any program having to do with children will generate popular support; one to do away with some particularly obnoxious slum area; anything that will help attract more customers to a struggling, older shopping area; or any sort of scheme that will make the community an attractive tourist mecca is likely to be enthusiastically endorsed and supported whereas a program to build an art gallery or enlarge a public library will be harder to promote, simply because this sort of project, though worthy, appeals to fewer people and may be regarded as a luxury the community cannot afford.

In evaluating the community survey and selecting a project the cost of future maintenance should never be overlooked. Firm commitments must be obtained from the local government if it is to take over the care of the project and, if not, some sort of adequate fund must be set up to take care of it much in the manner of perpetual-care funds in cemeteries. Nothing is more detrimental to the cause of civic improvement than some neglected, deteriorating project which was undertaken without concern for its future care.

Phase Two

The second phase of the project, the actual construction or carrying out of what has been planned, must be carefully organized. We must warn individuals or groups from trying to carry out the actual work with their own hands. This work should be assigned to the various trades and professionals who know how to do it, and who are paid for their work. The sponsoring committee should be responsible for generally overseeing the work and raising the money for it, but not for the actual, physical work of carrying it out.

Except on the smallest of projects, the use of volunteer labor contributed by the husbands of the committee members, the Boy Scouts, or whomever, is to be firmly deplored. These people, with the best will in the world, simply do not know how to lay brick, dig plants and replant them, or perform any of the many other tasks that must go into any operation of this sort. Let those who are interested contribute the skills they have, like speaking at meetings, raising money, cajoling public officials, shopping for prices of materials and labor and the like, but do not ask them to mix concrete, paint the town hall, or prepare a lawn area for seeding.

Anyone who has tried to get a project carried out by using volunteer labor will understand perfectly what we mean. Not only are volunteers unskilled in the particular work in hand, but they often fail to show up when needed, tire easily and quit regardless of how many plants remain unplanted or how much mortar lies mixed but unused. The person in charge of the work is sure to have to leave right in the middle of it to fetch the children from school or to do some other important errand that simply can't be put off. Part of the essential work of organizing a project is to arrange to have someone competent in charge of it at all times when the work is going on. Such a person should, of course, be paid for his time and knowledge just as a professional should be paid for any plans he may draw in connection with it. If these people voluntarily decide not to accept payment, all well and good, but this should not be expected of them.

During the course of the project's execution, frequent and well-documented reports should be furnished to cooperating or sponsoring agencies, not only because they have a right to such information but also to maintain their interest in it and to pave the way for future projects under their sponsorship or with their help. These reports should also be given to the publicity chairman who can often use them, together with pictures showing the progress of the work, the committee members, and other interesting items, as timely news topics in the press from time to time to stimulate general interest and continued support on the part of the public. Giving public credit through well-designed publicity to those who have contributed to the project in one way or another, particularly public officials, should never be neglected. These people may be again needed and such public acknowledgment of their part in civic beautification and development can help assure that their support will be available when needed.

If plans and specifications for the project have been carefully prepared, as we hope they will have been, the actual execution of the work can be entrusted to the various trades and mechanics involved. Someone from the sponsoring group or steering committee should, however, keep in close touch with the work to settle the minor difficulties that will always arise, to encourage the workers and to see that the plans and specifications are carried out as they should be without too much modification. In any construction job unforeseen problems will arise from time to time, and some minor adjustments will have to be made. This should disturb no one provided the spirit of the plans and specifications is not violated.

Phase Three

When the project is completed the third phase of the work follows. This should begin with some sort of ceremony or celebration calling the attention of the community to what has been accomplished. Never hide your light under a bushel! Take advantage of every opportunity for constructive publicity. Since names make news, and news is what is wanted at this point, get someone of prominence in the government, the arts, or finance to attend the ceremony, cut the ribbon, and speak a few well-chosen words. Make as big a show as possible within the bounds of good taste.

After this the job is to keep the project under constant surveillance to make sure that the money earmarked for its care continues to be made available from whatever source, and to see that the people who are doing the actual maintenance work know what they are up to. This is particularly important if the project involves trees and shrubs. Improper care of these can ruin a good project in no time, and turn it into an eyesore. If they are to grow successfully trees and shrubs must be fed, watered, and properly pruned. There are right and wrong ways of doing all these things. Whoever is in charge must be sufficiently knowledgeable not to make mistakes.

We have called attention to improper pruning in public

places and we repeat the warning. When shrubs become too large for their locations, as in time most shrubs do, they should be removed and be replaced. This continual replacement should be considered as a customary part of the maintenance program. Nothing should be allowed to get completely out of hand. The designer of the project had a certain composition of line, form, and texture in mind when he designed it. When plants grow, these relationships, especially scale, are distorted and many times plant materials need to be replaced with the same or very similar materials so that the original composition is not destroyed.

Structures as well as planting need careful maintenance. Wooden ones need occasional painting or staining, masonry ones need pointing up once in a while. Lettering on monuments and plaques needs to be kept clean so that it can be read. Playground equipment will wear out and must be replaced promptly. All public spaces must be kept clean and neat. All these tasks are part of the maintenance program and none of them may be safely overlooked.

In the beginning of this discussion we acknowledged that the task of civic improvement and beautification is a gigantic challenge to us all. How well we meet that challenge may be a measure of how effective we are as citizens. All of us are involved, but on those who actively take up the crusade against ugliness will fall most of the burdens, the disappointments, and heartaches, but also to them will come the satisfaction that arises only as a reward for a job well done. Those who have been through the experience know that this feeling of accomplishment far outweighs any and all difficulties met along the way. At the end one can regard one's work and say, with pride, "that *was* a job!"

HOW DOES YOUR TOWN RATE?

I. First Impressions:

    A. *Are the town approaches neat and uncluttered?* ——

        1. Are the highway verges well kept? ——

        2. Are there fine long-lived shade trees? ——

        3. Are there some well-located and selected shrub masses and groups of small ornamental trees? ——

        4. Are there objectionable billboards or signs? ——

        5. Are there shoddy roadside stands? ——

        6. Are there unscreened dumps? ——

        7. Are there automobile graveyards? ——

    B. *Is the town itself neat and uncluttered?* ——

        1. Are the streets, alleys, and rear yards clean? ——

        2. Are there unsightly utility poles and wires? ——

        3. Are the streets shaded by fine trees? ——

    C. *What is the outlook from hotel, motel, or restaurant windows?*

        1. Is it neat, tidy, and pleasing? ——

        2. Are there shade trees and other plantings where there is room for them? ——

II. More Detailed Impressions:

    A. *Do the residential areas give the impression that the people who live there are proud of their homes?* ——

        1. Are the houses tastefully designed, well painted and maintained? ——

        2. Are the grounds pleasing in over-all arrangement? ——

    B. *Are the commercial and industrial areas an asset?* ——

        1. Are the buildings and grounds well maintained? ——

        2. Are there plantings where there is space? ——

    C. *Are there parks?* ——

        1. Are they adequate in size and distribution? ——

    2. Are there plantings where there is space?   _____

    3. Are they well maintained?   _____

D. *Are there playgrounds?*   _____

    1. Are they adequate in size and well distributed?   _____

    2. Are they well equipped?   _____

    3. Are they used?   _____

    4. Are they well maintained?   _____

    5. Are new areas being reserved and developed?   _____

E. *Are the grounds around public and semipublic buildings such as library, municipal offices, or churches attractively developed?*   _____

    1. Are there trees and planting where there is space?   _____

    2. Is there adequate off-street parking?   _____

    3. Are these places well maintained?   _____

F. *Are the school grounds properly landscaped?*   _____

G. *Are the cemeteries well maintained?*   _____

H. *Planning and Zoning:*

    1. Has your town established a planning department?   _____

    2. Has it a zoning ordinance?   _____

    3. Has it a Board of Appeals for Zoning?   _____

    4. Has it subdivision controls?   _____

    5. Has it a tree ordinance?   _____

    6. Has it a sign ordinance?   _____

    7. Has it a building code?   _____

    8. Has it a supervised community dump?   _____

    9. Is the dump well maintained and screened?   _____

    10. Does the town have a refuse collection?   _____

    11. Does the town have adequate sewage disposal?   _____

    12. Does the highway department keep the streets clean?   _____

III. THESE EXTRAS MAKE YOUR TOWN OUTSTANDING:

A. *Has it a civic center?*   _____

    1. Is it well planned and planted?   _____

    2. Is it well maintained?   _____

B. *Has it a town or courthouse square?*   _____

    1. Is it well planned and planted?   _____

    2. Is it well maintained?   _____

3. Have you protected it from being encroached upon for parking? _____

4. Could it be improved by redesign? _____

C. *Are there other well-maintained squares where sculpture or other memorials are located?* _____

   1. Are these well designed and planted? _____

   2. Are they well maintained? _____

D. *Are there points of historical interest?* _____

   1. Have they been restored to their original condition? _____

   2. Are they well planted and maintained? _____

E. *Has your town made the most of oustanding natural features, lake, river, shoreline, etc.?* _____

   1. Have they been attractively developed? _____

   2. Are they well maintained? _____

   3. Are there any provisions for the acquisition of additional open space? _____

SUGGESTED ORGANIZATION TABLE FOR CIVIC BEAUTIFICATION PROGRAM

Honorary Chairman	Head of city government or influential citizen
General Chairman	A prominent citizen with adequate time to devote to program
Executive Chairman	The head of an Executive Committee made up of the heads of the following committees:
Chairman of Publicity Committee	Aided by 3–5 members connected with newspapers, radio, TV, and advertising or who have had experience in publicity
Chairman of Commerce Committee	Aided by 3–5 members selected from Chamber of Commerce, retail merchants, banks, public utilities, etc.
Chairman of Neighborhood Committee	Aided by 3–5 members form civic associations, service clubs, garden clubs, etc.
Chairman of Ways and Means Committee	Preferably a banker or treasurer of a corporation aided by 3–5 members with experience in fund raising
Chairman of Professional Committee	An architect or landscape architect aided by 3–5 members selected from the various professions including one from the legal profession

SUGGESTED PROJECTS

Areas to Be Considered for Design and Planting Programs:
  Bus stations and stops
  Cemeteries
  Entrances to airport
              fair grounds and parks
              railroad station
              town or city itself
  Highway clover-leaf intersections
              median strips
              rest areas
  Historic buildings
              markers
              sites
  Parks
  Parking lots
  Planting in business district
  Playgrounds
  Public buildings
  School grounds
  Screen planting for dumps and junkyards
              industrial areas
              superhighways
  Riverbanks
  Squares
  Street tree planting
  Street intersections
Community Projects Requiring Civic Action:
  Anti-litter campaign
  Clean-up campaign
  Sign ordinance
  Street tree ordinance
  Town planning and zoning
  Urban renewal
  Vacant lot clean-up
  Weed removal from highway verges

Bibliography

Anderson, Robert M., *Architectural Controls*. Reprint, Syracuse, N.Y., Law Review, 1960.

Eliot, Charles W., *Charles Eliot, Landscape Architect*. Boston, Houghton Mifflin Company, 1902.

Gallion, Arthur B., *The Urban Pattern*. New York, D. Van Nostrand Company, Inc., 1950.

Higbee, Edward, *The Squeeze*. New York, William Morrow & Company, Inc., 1960.

Hubbard, Alice H., *This Land of Ours*. New York, The Macmillan Company, 1960.

Morrison, Jacob H., *Historic Preservation Law*. New Orleans, Pelican Publishing Company, 1957.

Ortloff, H. Stuart, and Raymore, Henry B., *The Book of Landscape Design*. New York, M. Barrows & Company, Inc., 1959.

Udall, Stewart L., *The Quiet Crisis*. New York, Holt, Rinehart & Winston, 1963.

Conservation Education. PA 529, U.S. Department of Agriculture Forest Service, 1962.

Control of Land Subdivision. Bureau of Planning, Department of Commerce, Albany, N.Y.

Highlights in History of Forest Conservation. U.S. Department of Agriculture Forest Service.

Journal of the American Institute of Architects (publication). Washington, D.C.

Landscape Architecture (quarterly). American Society of Landscape Architects, Washington, D.C.

Landscape Design for Street Trees. Southern Bell Tel. & Tel. Co.

Newsletters. Pennsylvania Roadside Council, Inc., Media, Penna.

Planting Trees (bulletin). Union Electric, St. Louis, Mo.

Roadside Brush Control. Station Paper No. 148, Upper Darby,

Penna.; Northeastern Forest Experiment Station, U.S. Department of Agriculture Forest Service.

Selective Tree Planting (bulletin). Long Island Lighting Co., Mineola, N.Y.

Solving of Parking Problems. Department of Commerce, Albany, N.Y., 1950.

Trees Are Lovely (bulletin). Virginia Electric & Power Co., Richmond, Va.

Vanishing Natural Areas of the United States. The Nature Conservancy, Washington, D.C.

What's Happening Along Our Roadside. Connecticut Arboretum Association, Bulletin No. 13, Connecticut College, New London, Conn.

Zoning and Traffic. Eno Foundation for Highway Traffic Control, Saugatuck, Conn., 1952.

Assistance and helpful publications are available from:
Forest Service, U.S. Department of Agriculture, Washington 25, D.C.
Soil Conservation Service, U.S. Department of Agriculture, Washington 25, D.C.
U.S. Department of Health, Education and Welfare, Washington 25, D.C.
U.S. Department of the Interior, Washington 25, D.C.
Various State departments of Commerce, Conservation, etc.
County Agents or Extension Services of State universities

Also from the following organizations:
American Association of Nurserymen, 635 Southern Building, Washington 5, D.C.
American Society of Landscape Architects, 2000 K Street N.W., Washington 6, D.C.
Keep America Beautiful, Inc., 99 Park Avenue, New York 16, N.Y.
National Audubon Society, 1130 Fifth Avenue, New York 28, N.Y.
National Council of State Garden Clubs, Inc., 4401 Magnolia Avenue, St. Louis 10, Mo.
The Nature Conservancy, 2039 K Street, Washington 6, D.C.
Sierra Club, Mills Tower, San Francisco 4, Calif.

Index